Gotcha

Personal Anecdotes & Essays

Paul E. Linzey

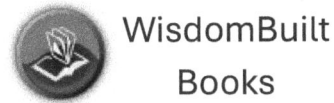

WisdomBuilt Books

GOTCHA

Copyright © 2025 Paul E. Linzey

All rights reserved. No part of this publication may be reproduced, distributed or transmitted in any form or by any means, including photocopying, recording, or other electronic or mechanical methods, without the prior written permission of the publisher or author.

The cover image is from Pixabay.com and is used by permission.

Scriptures taken from the Holy Bible, New International Version®, NIV®. Copyright © 1973, 1978, 1984, 2011 by Biblica, Inc.™ Used by permission of Zondervan. All rights reserved worldwide. www.zondervan.com The "NIV" and "New International Version" are trademarks registered in the United States Patent and Trademark Office by Biblica, Inc.™

Scripture taken from the Holman Christian Standard Bible®, Copyright © 1999, 2000, 2002, 2003 by Holman Bible Publishers. Used by permission. Holman Christian Standard Bible®, Holman CSB®, and HCSB® are federally registered trademarks of Holman Bible Publishers.

ISBN: 979-8-9863828-9-0

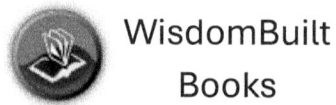

WisdomBuilt Books

GOTCHA

DEDICATION

To my brother, Dave

CONTENTS

1. Gotcha	1
2. Inspected by #1	3
3. Speed Bumps	6
4. When The Lights Go Out	10
5. Running a Marathon	12
6. Soiled Lives	14
7. What Did You Say?	19
8. Can Dreams Come True?	23
9. The Annual Newsletter	27
10. Traffic Light in Boston	30
11. Boy in the Fountain	34
12. The Power of Forgiveness	37
13. Being Spiritual Together	39
14. The Power of the Tongue	42
15. Jack Reacher and Marriage	45
16. The Ukrainian Officer	48
17. My Fiery Furnace	51
18. The Risk of Faith	54
19. Unity Produces Winners	57
20. When the Ship Sinks	60
21. He's Na Heavy; He's Mi Brither	63
22. Heat, Danger, Dust, and Death	66
23. In a Hurry and Running Late	68
24. E-5 for Life	71
25. Metamorphosis	75
26. Man of the House	77

CONTENTS

27. A Turkish Proverb		79
28. The Old Chevy		82
29. Yada, Yada, Yada		85
30. Light of the World		89
31. Arizona Pothole		92
32. The Chemistry of Falling in Love		95
33. Driving with a Bad Attitude		98
34. The Wisdom of Whales		101
35. Rest from Pain and Rest from Wrong		104
36. Invisible Forces		107
37. The Finest Hours		110
38. Selma		113
39. Only a Receptionist		114
40. Show Me the Money		117
41. Watering the Pineapple		120
42. Strawberry Pie		123
43. God is Our Helper		125
44. First Breath		128
45. Walking the Beagle		130
46. Ancient Canine Ritual		132
47. What It Means to Be a Man		135
Acknowledgements		138
About the Author		139
Books by Paul Linzey		141

INTRODUCTION

My brother, Dave, has been instrumental in my spiritual growth and maturity most of my life. It began when he was fourteen and I was fifteen.

As a sophomore in high school, I started reading the Bible regularly and tried to get serious about being a Christian. The problem was that I was inconsistent. There were too many times when I was unkind, rude, perhaps even hypocritical. What made it worse was that I was blind to my own weaknesses, while really good at pointing out the faults in others.

Even as a teen, Dave had a keen insight into people's thoughts, motivations, and behaviors, and he stopped calling me by my name. Suddenly, the new name he gave me was "Holy Cow."

"Why do you call me that?" I asked.

"Because you're a hypocrite," he answered matter-of-factly. You claim to be so spiritual but you're phony. You're not real." His words stung, but he was right.

As an adult, Dave was determined to be genuine, authentic, and self-actualized, and he continued to help me grow in that direction. Sometimes by speaking to me, other times by example. Whether by text, a phone call, or in person, he would let me know when something I said or wrote came across as being critical, judgmental, or condemning. Then he would ask, "Is that what you want to communicate?"

GOTCHA

This collection of articles, essays, and blogs covers a lot of themes, many of them religious, others practical, and some dealing with relationships. A few even focus on my Beagle.

It is not my intent to condemn or judge anyone, so if you see that or feel that in any of the pieces, please don't blame my brother. And please believe me when I say that's not my intent. Hopefully, the first anecdote will set a tone of loving people unconditionally and caring about them.

With that in mind, I just want to say to my brother, "Gotcha."

1
GOTCHA

Early in my military career, I showed up at a new infantry battalion one day and started meeting some of the guys. The Sergeant Major introduced himself and asked, "Hey Chaplain, do you have your Gotcha Cards?"

"No, Sergeant Major. I've never heard of a Gotcha Card, and don't know what it is, so I'm pretty sure I don't have one. What is it?"

"Our previous chaplain, every time he heard one of us cuss or swear or use the Lord's name in vain would pull out a business card, but all it said in big bold letters was GOTCHA. So when the guys heard we were getting a new chaplain, they started wondering if you were going to be like the last one."

"I bet you guys hated him."

"Yes. We. Did."

"Tell you what. I'm not planning on having any Gotcha Cards printed up, so you can relax. Cuss if you want. I'm just here to love you guys."

Apparently, a bunch of Soldiers were listening to

the conversation, because as soon as I made that last statement, a cheer erupted from around the corner.

"You're gonna fit in fine here, Chaps. Nice to have you aboard."

Over the next two years, I led more than 25 of those guys to faith in Christ, and I never once said, GOTCHA. Oh, they cussed, alright. But I figured it was the Holy Spirit's job to reach them, and he does a pretty good job. I just had to do my part, which was love them and be consistent in setting an example of what a Christian is and does.

2
INSPECTED BY #1

Have you ever found an "Inspected By" tag when you bought new clothes? One day I came home with a jacket, and when I reached into the pocket to look for that little slip of paper, I was surprised when it said, "Inspected By #1." The first thing that went through my mind was, "Whoa! The top dude inspected my coat!"

When God created the universe and everything in it, he "looked over all he had made, and he saw that it was very good!" Genesis 1:31

Then he attached the little tag that says, "Inspected by #1." He did the same thing when he made you. He slipped that little tag in the pocket of your life that says, "Inspected By #1." The fact of the matter is this: God loves you and treasures you.

Most of us look at ourselves with a distorted or twisted perspective. We either see ourselves as no-good dirty rotten scoundrels with nothing good about us, or we see ourselves through rose-colored glasses, without any faults, weaknesses, or blemishes.

But when we look at Psalm 139, we begin to understand how God sees us, and his perspective is objective, fair, and accurate. He sees us as we really are. He knows everything about us, both good and bad, yet he loves us. Listen to a few verses from the Psalm.

You have searched me, Lord, and you know me. You know when I sit and when I rise; you perceive my thoughts from afar. You discern my going out and my lying down; you are familiar with all my ways. . . . For you created my inmost being; you knit me together in my mother's womb; I praise you because I am fearfully and wonderfully made; your works are wonderful, I know that full well. . . . all the days ordained for me were written in your book before one of them came to be. Psalms 139:1-5, Psalms 139:13-16

If I am to have a healthy and accurate view of myself, it's helpful to understand how God sees me. The same is true for you. Only when we see through God's eyes do we really see ourselves honestly. Then, we discover that nobody is all bad, and nobody is all good. Each of us has some wonderful qualities and characteristics, and each of us has some attributes that are not very attractive. Some of these traits get in the way of our becoming who and what we were created to be and hinder us from developing a relationship with the Lord and with other people.

These verses from Psalm 139 fill me with hope. When I start beating myself up because I see myself as worthless, instead, I choose to focus on God's view of me. He knows every flaw, yet he loves me completely. I used to think God should love me less because of all my failures. Now, I realize that he pours out His love and grace on me just the way I am.

It's not always easy, but I'm getting better at seeing myself through God's eyes. For example. When I start taking on too many projects, maybe it's because I'm trying to prove that I'm worthy of God's love. So, I remind myself that I don't have to earn God's approval. Neither do you.

God knows you and loves you unconditionally. Yes, he sees the ways you have failed. He knows your imperfections. But he also sees your beauty, your qualities, and your potential.

An expert photographer takes a picture with an aesthetic eye, then crops, adjusts, or edits in order to create the desired effect, or to highlight a particular aspect of the photo. In the same way, God wants to highlight what is good in you. He wants to fully develop what he sees in you. And when he is done, he'll put that little slip of paper into your pocket: "Inspected by #1."

3
SPEED BUMPS

There were four or five speed bumps on the road ahead, but what caught my attention was the car in front of me. As it approached each bump in the road, it veered way over to the right to go around it. Didn't slow down. Just avoided the speed bumps.

I don't mind speed bumps. They don't bother me or my car in the least. Unless they are particularly obnoxious, or unless my wife is in the car with me, I go right over them without worrying. Without slowing very much, either, I must confess.

When the car ahead got to the last speed bump, there was a parked car on the side of the road, so the driver had no choice but to go over the bump. To accomplish this feat, he came to a complete stop. Then he crawled over the speed bump as if his car might be damaged if it went more than 2 MPH over that obstacle. It was a fairly new car, and it didn't seem fragile. Yet he crept over that speed bump as if his very life depended on not going any faster than the snail on the sidewalk next to him. The earthworm on the other side sped past him. Just zipped on by!

I watched the scene play out, trying to remain patient. I had a meeting to attend, but I could wait a little longer to see what the fellow would do. See if his jalopy would survive the ordeal of climbing over that mountain. It got all the way to the top of the speed bump and eased down the other side. Then the driver looked around, breathed a heavy sigh of relief, and accelerated. He was a success. A survivor. He was having a good day!

After the meeting, I thought about the speed bump episode. We all face bumps in the road in everyday life. Sometimes we call them hiccups or obstacles. Some people refuse to use the word "problem," preferring, instead, to call them "challenges." But they're real.

Jesus said plainly in John 16:33 that there'll be trouble, sorrow, pain, and difficulty in this world. Different translations of the Bible use words like tribulation, trials, distress, and afflictions. The Greek word is thlipsis, which refers to a variety of tough circumstances.

The fact is, life is tough. And just when you think it's going to ease up a bit, it gets harder. It tests your faith. It raises hard questions. It makes you want to run away. "But be of good cheer," the Lord goes on to say. "Take heart, be brave, don't let it defeat you."

Jesus knew about hardship. He knew what it

meant to suffer, to hurt, to wish things could turn out differently. So did James, who wrote that we can be joyful even when going through tough stuff, knowing that the Lord is at work in our lives. So did Paul, who said God was working for our good in every situation. Even when hitting those speed bumps.

Years ago, in a pick-up game of basketball, the other team got a rebound and was running a 4-on-1 fast break. Trying to defend them, I turned to reach for the ball. In doing so, I twisted my knee, snapped my ACL, and landed on the ground in pain. Surgery was followed by months of physical therapy.

To this day, I have an awareness and a compassion for people who have a leg, knee, or foot injury. Whenever I see someone in a wheelchair, on crutches, or wearing a knee brace, I remember what it was like falling to the ground in agony, then being helped off the court by friends. For a moment, I relive the exercises designed to restore strength and range of motion. My painful experience helped me become more aware of other people and what they're going through.

We can't avoid speed bumps, can't always drive around them like the guy in front me was trying to do. There will always be problems, challenges, and obstacles. Some will be overwhelming, others mere hiccups. What we can do is face them with courage, patience, and confidence, staying open to the idea that they just might lead to personal growth and maturity, and just maybe help us develop a sense of compassion and an ability to relate to other people.

4
WHEN THE LIGHTS GO OUT

It was Friday night, we'd gone out for dinner, and barely made it back into the garage before the downpour.

When the power went off, I was writing at my computer and my wife was reading an ebook on her tablet. The plan was to watch a movie a little later, but there we were with no electricity, no lights, no internet, and no television.

"What do we do now," she asked.

I reached into the desk drawer for the flashlight that doubles as a cell phone power source, plugged in my phone, and turned on the mobile hotspot so we could maintain internet connection. Then I walked over to the kitchen pantry where we keep two battery-operated camping lanterns, pulled one out, and placed it on the kitchen counter, where its light sprayed throughout the kitchen, dining room, and living room. Not a lot, but enough.

For the next hour, rain poured from the sky as if God had picked up the Atlantic Ocean and was dumping it on us. Linda took the lantern over to the couch to read; my laptop had plenty of charge for me to finish the work I was doing.

Although the rest of the house was dark, and the temperature grew warmer because the air conditioner was off, we didn't have a crisis when the lights went out. During the previous weekend, we had checked the batteries in those emergency lamps and charged my mobile power back-up. Because we were ready, there was no emergency when the storm caused a blackout. We didn't panic, and there wasn't a crisis.

The same can be true if something terrible happens and life itself comes to an end. If we've taken time to prepare in advance, even death isn't a crisis, and we don't have to panic. In Philippians 1:21 the Apostle writes, to live is Christ, and to die is gain. That doesn't sound like a man who is afraid of the dark or of death. He was prepared for whatever might happen. Job is another who had a deep confidence when facing the storms of life. Despite all the pain and ugliness that he faced, he still declared, I know that my Redeemer lives (Job 19:25).

When the lights finally came back on, we watched an old Alfred Hitchcock movie starring James Stewart and Doris Day. It was a lovely evening—despite the storm raging on the outside.

5
RUNNING A MARATHON

Nobody shows up the day of a marathon without taking the time, the effort, and the expense to get ready, because running a marathon requires months of preparation. The training has to include long distances several days a week. Eating habits need to be modified because nutrition can work for or against the body and the mind.

A marathoner will become an expert on things like foot care, clothing, and how to prevent chafing. Research will determine the best shoes for the particular shape of the foot and the unique way each athlete runs. Just as important is the training of the mind for the grueling ordeal of running 26.2 miles, because anyone who loses the mental game is already in trouble.

Another aspect of preparing for the race is being careful to stretch and warm up before every run. This is crucial in the prevention of injury. It also enables the runner to extend the stride for maximum reach, which equates to more ground covered each step of the way, and when running 26 miles, an inch or two per stride adds up, which means less time to complete the race, and a greater chance of winning the race.

The same attention to detail must be considered when preparing for life, marriage, a career, or ministry. Putting in the time to pray, do the research, and count the cost will pave the way for long-term success. And in the same way a runner will stretch before running, the Christian will stretch and warm up spiritually every day. This is done by reading the Bible, singing a few worship songs, or spending time in the presence of the Lord. This daily "quiet time" enables you to reach a little farther each step of the way, just like stretching helps lengthen the runner's stride. And it helps prevent spiritual or emotional injury, the same way stretching prevents physical injury.

In the big picture, this daily practice will enable you to proclaim with the apostle in 2 Timothy 4:7: I have fought the good fight, I have finished the race, I have kept the faith (HCSB).

We never know what we might face in the future. That's why it's so important to continually add to our training, our learning, and our growing, both personally and professionally. The price of success is high, and we have to count the cost. Is it worth it? You have to decide for yourself. On your mark. Get set. Go!

6
SOILED LIVES

When I answered the phone, it was my uncle. Though he had sons of his own and I had a father, he always called me "Son."

"Son, I understand you want to be a pastor?"

"Yes, sir."

"So you think you're called, huh?"

"Yes, sir. I do."

"Son, if you are really called to the ministry, meet me at the church Thursday morning and spend the day with me."

My classes at San Diego State were on Monday-Wednesday-Friday, so Thursday morning I got up and went to the church. I had no idea what he had in mind. After chatting for a few minutes, he said, "Follow me." We got into his car and, without saying a word, drove to the outskirts of town, pulled up to a cluster of tiny, two-room shacks, and parked on the dirt in front of a small green hut, too small to be called a house or an apartment, yet this was someone's home.

Uncle got out of the car, and I followed. We walked up to the door of one of the units, and he knocked. No answer. He knocked again, louder this time. Again, no answer. "I know he's in there."

He tried the door and found that it was unlocked. Slowly he opened it and went in. There on the bed in the small two-room cabin was a man: drunk, passed out, a mixture of vomit, diarrhea, urine, and alcohol on the bed, walls, sofa, and floor. The stench was overwhelming, as if attacking my nostrils and throat. I thought I was going to throw up.

Without saying a word, without even a grimace, Uncle took off his suit coat and tie, and handed them to me. I watched as the man of God took on the role of the servant. He turned on the water to fill the tub, then went over to the bed. He undressed the man, rolled up his putrid clothing, and placed them into a garbage bag. He picked up the still-unconscious drunkard, naked and filthy, placed him carefully into the tub, and bathed him. I thought of the scene in the Gospel of John where Peter said to the Lord, Wash all of me. Not just part of me.

After washing the man, who never did wake up, he said to me, "Watch him to make sure he doesn't drown." Then he went back to the bed, stripped it of the blankets and sheets, and put those into the bag with the clothes. Finding an old towel, he mopped the walls and the floor, repeatedly going over to the sink to rinse the crud away. He searched the dresser drawers til he found a set of clean sheets and a blanket, and made the bed. There was a fresh pair of pajamas in a drawer, and he placed them on the end of the bed.

After cleaning up the place, my uncle returned to the bathroom, dried off the comatose body, carried him to the bed, and put the pajamas on him. He covered him up and tucked him in, then he took the bag of soiled clothing, bed linens, and a few other things that needed to be laundered, walked out to the car, and put them in the trunk of his car.

After locking the man's door, we got into the car. The foul smell was not confined to the trunk of the car. It filled the passenger compartment as well. The stench came with us, not only because of the awful stuff in the trunk, but because the filth had gotten onto my uncle's suit. Although by now it was almost time for lunch, I thought I was going to lose my breakfast.

Instead of going back to the church, we drove to the pastor's home, where he took the bag from the trunk, went straight to the laundry room, and washed the man's clothes and bed linens. After showering, my uncle dressed, and we went back to the church. Before I got into my car to go home, he said to me, "Son, that's what ministry is all about. Good people soil themselves and make a mess of their lives because of sin. Your job as a pastor is to find out what Jesus wants you to do about it. And then do it."

Though my uncle is no longer alive, I never

forgot him . . . or that lesson. As we go about the daily tasks that the Lord has called us to do, sometimes we find ourselves cleaning up our own messes, sometimes the messes other people have made. The ugly scenes are often the result of sin, our own or someone else's. Some of the mountains of debris we are called to help clean up are caused by years of neglect, ignorance, discouragement, abuse, or failure.

In Lakeland, Florida, at the center of Southeastern University's campus, is a bronze sculpture of Jesus washing the feet of one of his disciples. The sculpture is titled "Divine Servant." It is a great work of art, beautifully depicting the call for genuine disciples to be servant ministers. Ironically, the sculpture is beautiful, whereas the brokenness of human lives is quite unattractive, and working with broken people can get ugly. When I see it, I can't help but think of my uncle.

In his book, Facing Messy Stuff in the Church, Ken Swetland talks about the ugly, painful situations church leaders have to deal with. "Churches are made up of sinners whose lives are broken – sometimes because of their own choices, sometimes because of experiencing wrongs outside of their control." He goes on to write that the church is ". . . a fellowship of people who come together to worship God, serve him in the world, and be agents of healing in the lives of broken people who make up the church."

As we respond to the situations that people have

made of their lives, their families, their cities, or their nation, it is helpful to keep in mind that we have a rich heritage of serving in Jesus' name, cleaning up the stench and the debris of people's lives. As my uncle said, that's what ministry is all about.

7
WHAT DID YOU SAY?

Wife:	"I said, the test came out positive."
Husband:	"Positive?"
Wife:	"The home pregnancy test I got at the grocery store."
Husband:	"What?"
Wife:	"I told you about it."
Husband:	"If you did, I wasn't paying attention."
Wife:	"We're going to have a baby!"
Husband:	"Oh my!"
Wife:	"Aren't you happy about it?"
Husband:	"Yeah . . . Sure . . . I mean . . ."
Wife:	"What's the matter?"
Husband:	"Are we ready for this?"
Wife:	"I think so."
Husband:	"Can we afford a baby?"
Wife:	"No."

GOTCHA

Husband:	"I don't even know how to take care of a baby."
Wife:	"I do. And you'll learn."
Husband:	"I don't feel grown up enough to be a parent."
Wife and	"We'll grow into the roles of Mommy Daddy."
Husband:	"Are you sure you're pregnant?"
Wife:	"Take a look for yourself."

Eight months later, our son was born. I'd never changed a diaper. Never had a crying baby wake me up in the middle of the night. Never imagined my wife saying, "It's your turn to feed him." Never fathomed the immensity of the changes about to take place.

Life as we knew it was over. Sleeping through the night? Never again! Date night? No babysitter. Watch a TV show all the way through, uninterrupted? Fat chance!

My wife did most of the childcare duties. But there were times I was in charge. Well, that's overly optimistic. No father is ever "in charge" of a baby. It's a matter of survival for both of us. "OK, kiddo. Let's watch the football game." Three hours later Mommy comes home and finds a crying baby who hasn't been fed or changed and me glued to the TV set. Well, let's just say it wasn't a fun conversation.

We had a family reunion, and all the ladies went out to lunch together, leaving the men and children behind. My son had the nerve to poop his diaper.

When I asked my older, wiser, more experienced brother-in-law (who I thought was my friend) if he'd change my son's diaper, he laughed at me. "The kid is yours; you gotta do it." I thought I was going to throw up. And my wife does this every day?

Several months later, our son was screaming in the middle of a sleepless night. I remember praying that God would heal him and deliver him from teething. It was a genuine test of my theological position on faith, prayer, and whether God still does miracles. "Lord, I know you answer prayer. I know you can heal. Says so right there in the Bible? Heal that kid's gums right now in the name of Jesus!" It didn't work.

My wife had to work, so I took him to the pediatrician. The doctor told me to use whiskey. Seriously, that's what he said. "Use a little whiskey, and he won't feel the pain." Now, I'd seen a few westerns where the doc gives the guy a bottle of whiskey, and after the patient is drunk, the doc does the operation, amputates the leg, or removes the bullet. I actually thought our pediatrician was suggesting that we put some whiskey in the baby bottle, getting the kid slightly tipsy, so he won't feel a thing.

"I'm not giving my son whiskey, no sirree!"

"Silly man," my wife said. "The doctor meant rub it on his gums."

"How was I supposed to know that?"

We went to the drug store and loaded up on Oragel, Liquid Tylenol, and Teething Biscuits. My wife was very careful about how much painkiller to give our son, and for some reason, she'd get mad at me for giving him too much.

"What do you mean, I give him too much. If a little bit is good for him, then doubling or tripling the dose is even better. What's wrong with that?"

She forbade me from ever giving the baby his medicine. In actuality, I'm pretty sure her intent was to forbid me from being a parent ever again!

We went to a parenting seminar, where the psychologist said, "Being parents of babies and toddlers is the most difficult time in your life. You feel like you're going crazy. You have no adult conversation and no friends. You're not getting any sleep. Hang in there, because the baby will grow up and you'll have a life again." Those were the most encouraging words we ever heard.

Our son was growing up. He started walking. Then talking. But he had a problem stuttering. My brother, who was a counselor, suggested that we slow down our own speech. "Your son might be trying to talk as fast as you guys, and he just can't do it. Slow down when you talk and see if it helps." So, we tried it, and within a week, his stuttering stopped.

A few months later, I came home from work one day, and my wife had a funny look on her face as she was muttering.

"What did you say?"

"I said the test came out positive."

"Noooooooooooooooo!"

8
CAN DREAMS COME TRUE?

A question often asked by people around the world is whether dreams can come true. Of course, it depends on what kind of dreams we're talking about.

When I was a kid, I often dreamed about finding buried coins in the front yard. Lots of money, usually quarters and dimes. When I was eight or nine, this dream was so real that in the dream, I took all the loot, wrapped it up, and hid it in my bottom dresser drawer so it would all be there when I woke up in the morning. I was so disappointed when I woke up the next day, ran over to my dresser, opened it, only to find that there was no money. I used to have that dream three or four times a year up until I was about thirty. Now it's only once every other year or so. It never has come true.

Then there's the dream where I'm in school or at church or some other public location, and all I have on is my underwear. Interestingly, in this dream, even though I am totally embarrassed, nobody else ever even seems to notice. Fortunately, this dream has never come true, either.

After returning from the war in Iraq, I frequently had dreams and nightmares for the next two years or so. Explosions, gunfire, or dangerous situations. What a relief when those gradually faded away. It's been several years now. The only two aspects of PTSD that still linger are the claustrophobia and eating in a hurry. I can't seem to overcome those.

But there are some dreams that really do come true. Let me tell you about three of them.

Several years ago, my wife and I were invited to teach a three-week intensive class at the Hungarian Bible College in Budapest. We taught the class every morning, then in the evenings and weekends, would preach in churches in Budapest and nearby towns.

One day, our missionary hosts had to go up to Czechoslovakia (now Czech and Slovak) for meetings with their regional supervisor, and told us how to get from their home to the college. The trip would require a bus ride part of the way, then the subway, and then we had to walk the rest of the way. Of course, the trip would be reversed after the class in order to get back to their home.

Up to this point, we had resisted taking the subway because the missionaries had told us about an American pastor who got lost in the metro. He had missed the station where he was supposed to get off and rode the train all the way to the end.

Seven hours later, he called to ask them to come and get him.

When we got to the subway, there was a huge, long escalator that took us way, way down. Longest escalator I have ever seen. When we finally reached bottom and turned right, I stopped. This was really strange, because the scene in front of me was familiar.

"Linda, I've been here before."

"What are you talking about? We've never been to Budapest."

"I know that, but I've seen this before." It was a really eerie feeling.

"How could you have seen this before?"

"I don't know. But if this is what I've seen before, the subway cars will come from the right, and they'll be blue."

In about fifteen seconds, the train arrived . . . from the right . . . and it was blue. We go in, the doors close, and the freaky experience continues.

"When we get to the next stop, the doors on the left will open, and the walls will all be yellow." Sure enough, that's what happened.

Even Linda was weirded out by now. "What's going on?"

"I don't know! But at the next stop, the doors on the left will open and the walls will be orange. But when we get to where we need to get off, the doors on the right will open, and the walls will be blue." It all unfolded exactly as I expected.

Then it dawned on me. Even though I had never

been in a subway, a year-and-a-half before we came to Hungary, I had a dream about being in this very subway, and the details in that dream were exactly the same as the reality we were now experiencing. That was a dream that came true.

Another dream I had as a kid was to be a Navy chaplain like my dad. But by the time I was ready to become a chaplain, the Lord redirected, I went into the Army instead, and had a wonderful, twenty-four-year career. Six years after retiring from the Army, I was invited to serve as the Protestant pastor at the Naval Academy in Annapolis, Maryland, working with the chaplains. It was a one-year assignment, but a fantastic experience. I felt like I had come full-circle back to my dream of being a Navy chaplain.

One more dream worth mentioning here, was the dream of growing up, falling in love, and marrying the woman of my dreams. That's another dream that came true. Life with Linda has been everything I had hoped for . . . and then some.

9
THE ANNUAL NEWSLETTER

Annual Newsletters: you've seen them, so you know the format. A recap of what happened during the year. Pictures that coincide with the stories. Almost always, the newsletter focuses on the good and fun events that happened during the year: the vacation, the promotion, the positives. We get them from friends and relatives every year, usually during the month of December. You get them too. You probably even sent a few.

But what do you do when only bad happens during the year? Do you still send out that festive, upbeat newsletter? This happened to us a few years ago. Right after Thanksgiving, my wife asked, "Are you doing a newsletter this year?"

"Yeah, sure. I'll tell all our friends what a crummy year we had."

When we recounted all the painful experiences and disappointments that happened during the year, we started laughing. That year, my wife gave up a job she really loved in order to be with me when the Army transferred me to a different part of the country. While there, she was diagnosed with cancer and had multiple surgeries. As she was recovering and going through chemotherapy, the Army sent me overseas, so I couldn't even be with her. That same year, I had an evil boss who was trying to destroy my career. One of our sons was unemployed, and our other two sons were struggling with personal issues. Bad news after bad news piled on top of us, and it seemed there was no end.

We have a pretty good idea how Job felt when he experienced horrible losses back-to-back-to-back, one after another. No wonder he groaned and grumbled and grieved. No wonder his wife suggested that he simply curse God and die. When life gets too painful and it seems there's no end to the suffering and bad news, there's not much you can do. We understand, because it happened to us.

But Job didn't turn his back on God. He didn't lose his faith. He didn't curse. And he didn't end his life. In fact, Job 1:22 indicates that in all his suffering, he didn't do anything wrong. He didn't end his life, he didn't sin, and he didn't blame God.

In our worst year ever, we adopted similar goals. We wanted to keep our eyes on Jesus and stay faithful in every way. When the world would advise us to give up, curse God, and die, we refused. And by the end of the year, even though we hadn't yet seen the light at the end of the tunnel in those dreadful situations, we managed to laugh together.

James 1:2-4 reminds us to remain joyful even when facing many kinds of trials, knowing that the testing of our faith produces character, perseverance, and strength. 1 Peter 4:12-13 adds that we shouldn't even be surprised when life gets ugly, as if something strange were happening. Instead, we can continue to be joyful, knowing that our Lord suffered too, keeping in mind that if we are faithful during the tough days, the Glory of the Lord will eventually be revealed in us.

Job knew this a long time ago, which is why he could proclaim, I know that my Redeemer lives, and in the end, He will stand. And then he adds, And I will see Him with my own eyes.

The same is true for you, my friend. Do your best to remain joyful and faithful while you're struggling, and you will see the glory of the Lord, because your Redeemer lives.

10
TRAFFIC LIGHT IN BOSTON

The station wagon with the third seat facing the rear pulled into Boston. My two younger brothers and I rode that seat from California to Massachusetts, watching where we'd been, rather than where we were going. 3,177 miles backwards. For a while I was dizzy, car sick, nauseous, but after a while I got used to it.

The '59 Dodge was a big car. It seemed like Mom and Dad, and whoever else was sitting up front with them, were in a different county. The actual dimensions of this monstrous car? Just over eighteen feet long, six-and-a-half feet wide, weighing about 4,200 pounds. The advertised top speed was 120 MPH, but I never saw my parents drive faster than 115. Mom liked to drive fast. I remember when it was my turn to sit up front and help her "stay awake" one night, driving through the Arizona desert while Dad got some sleep. It was scary.

GOTCHA

We got about nine miles per gallon if one or two people were in the car. Seven or eight miles a gallon when all ten of us went somewhere together, like we did on this cross-country trip. Nobody had seat belts back then.

As we pulled up to a traffic light in this strange city far from home, suddenly, my dad was yelling and talking excitedly. Someone outside was shouting and talking just as fast. From way back in the third row, I tried to see what was going on. Were my dad and the stranger mad at each other? Why were they yelling? I looked out the side window of our car and saw that the driver of the car next to us had dark skin and black curly hair. Why was he yelling at my dad? And why was my dad yelling back at him?

At first, it seemed they were angry with each other. But no, they weren't upset. Rather they were excited and happy. They were yelling for joy. But why?

As I kept on looking at the man in the car next to us, I glanced down to see the license plate on his car. We had played the license plate game all across the country: keep track of all the license plates and see who gets the most states. There were a lot of variations to that game; you've probably played something similar.

Riding backwards made it easier if the cars catching up to us had front license plates, because looking backwards I could see them before my brothers and sisters in the middle seat could see them. But if we were passing the other cars, then they got to see the license plates first. The way my parents drove, nobody ever passed us, so I never won the game.

At the red light in Boston, the license plate on the car next to us looked familiar. Was it? Yes! It was orange and black, a California license plate! We hadn't seen one of those since we left home. Was that why Dad and the other guy were hollering? Yep, sure was.

There we were, our first day in Boston. We didn't know a single soul in the city, or in the entire state of Massachusetts. But that first traffic light we stopped at in Boston placed us right next to another human being from California. It was his first day in Boston too.

It was my first memory of encountering an African-American, and the thing that stuck in my mind more than anything else was the connection that he and my dad made with each other. It wasn't age: my dad was forty-two and the other guy seemed to be younger. It wasn't family circumstance: my dad had a wife and eight kids in the car, while the other guy was single. It wasn't that they had similar careers: my dad was in the Navy, and the other guy worked in a factory. And it wasn't that they looked alike: my dad was a balding white guy, and the other guy was black with a full afro.

No, the connection they made with each other was simply that they had something in common. They were both from California, and that was enough. They were both more than 3,000 miles from home, and friendless . . . until that moment. But now, they found someone from home.

I often think about that experience. Why is it that people who are different despise each other? Why do people of different skin color or different nationality or different language or different gender or different religion or different political party or different socioeconomic standing hate each other? Why can't we do what my dad and the stranger did in Boston that day in 1962?

I was seven years old when we drove into Boston. Over the past sixty-plus years, I've tried to focus on what I have in common with other people, instead of our differences: marriage, kids, jobs, sports, music, food, weather, fears, dreams, movies, faith, or our human-ness. There's so much we share, and it's a shame people choose to fight over their differences.

Something powerful and amazing happens when we connect over something we have in common.

11
BOY IN THE FOUNTAIN

The little boy sat in the water directly on top of a water spout, cooling off from the heat. He looked to be about two years old.

He loved the feel of the cold water, contrasted with the hundred-degree temperature of the day. There were other children in the fountain: running, splashing, yelling, having fun. But this little guy just sat there. He didn't need much; just to be there was enough. I asked around until I found his mother, and got permission to take a picture. I didn't want her to think I meant any harm. I mentioned that I had children and grandchildren, and I thought her son was adorable. She looked at me, hesitated, then nodded.

I showed the photo to a few friends and heard comments like Cute, Adorable, Smart boy, Awww, and Can I Adopt Him?

I still wonder about him from time to time.

What's his life like? What's his family like? Where does he live now? Does he ever go back to that fountain?

And I wonder about his future, too. What will become of him? Will he like school? What sports will he want to play? What kind of music will he listen to? What does he want to do when he grows up? Although that may change a hundred times during his childhood.

Then, in light of recent stories in the news, I wonder if he'll turn out to be a good kid who grows into a fine young man, or if he'll get into trouble along the way. Will he ever be shot at by a gang, a friend, or a policeman? These thoughts are very real in America these days, and I wonder about this little guy.

I also wonder about my own grandchildren. I know their interests, their likes and dislikes, their preferences, what they want to be when they grow up. My eight-year-old granddaughter wants to be a doctor. Her five-year-old brother wants to be Buzz Lightyear or Spiderman, depending on the time of day, of course. They love school and learning. They love being part of a congregation of faith. They love playing family games. Life hasn't turned ugly for them, yet. But it could. Hate is a powerful force in America. Racism is still prevalent. Unkindness lurks.

I wonder how they might turn out, too. Will they fulfill their dreams? Will they get into trouble? Will they ever be the victims of prejudice? Will they have to defend themselves simply because their skin is darker, or their hair gives them away? Might they be subject to racial profiling some day? So far, they trust adults, those in authority, such as teachers, pastors, and police officers. Will they ever find their trust betrayed? Will they ever be afraid of being shot by someone they trust?

When I finished my lunch appointment and walked back to my car, the little boy was gone. His mother must have decided he'd been in the fountain long enough. He probably needed lunch. Perhaps it was nap time. Maybe she needed to go to work.

12
THE POWER OF FORGIVENESS

When you forgive, you release yourself and the other person from the pain and wrongs of your joint past. But forgiveness doesn't happen quickly. According to Christian ethicist Lewis Smedes, it happens slowly, with a little understanding, and sometimes with some confusion, because it has to sort out the anger and the injustice. When forgiveness has finished its work, however, both the forgiver and the offender have been renewed, transformed, and set free from the pain of the past.

Sometimes, you have to forgive the person you're still in relationship with because there's been unfaithfulness, a betrayal, neglect, or abuse. This is hard, but with God's help, and sometimes the help of a good pastor, counselor, or friend, you can be successful at putting the past behind you and moving forward in a fresh start.

Forgiveness doesn't mean there will be no scars.

GOTCHA

You carry the consequences of pain long after the hurting stops and the forgiveness is complete. The Christian singing group Point of Grace has a song that talks about the impact of the ugliness, pain, and shame of the past, which are often followed by scars that remain for a lifetime. Heal the Wound, written by Clint Lagerberg and Nicole Nordeman, focuses on the metaphor that even after an injury has healed, there's often a scar that lasts a lifetime. But instead of seeing the scar as a negative, they reframe it as a reminder of how gracious the Lord was in bringing you through the struggle.

13
BEING SPIRITUAL TOGETHER

Early in our marriage, at a time when my wife and I were really busy, with three kids at home, finances that were really tight, and a life filled with stress, we didn't know about the connection between spirituality and happiness in marriage. What we did know was that because of our circumstances, we got out of the habit of reading our Bibles, praying together, and taking time to worship together. We were totally unaware of the invisible toll it was taking.

We were snippy with each other, which isn't usually the case. We didn't have much patience. And, I was facing some strong sexual temptations. In the middle of this chapter of our lives, Linda said to me one day, "You know, we haven't prayed together or done family devotions in several weeks. I wonder if that's part of why we're struggling."

She was right. Almost as soon as we reinstated

our spiritual disciplines, a sense of unity was restored, we got along better, and the other circumstances were much easier to handle.

Couples who are active in their spiritual life together have a much higher rate of marital success. The opposite is also true. Couples who don't practice their faith together tend to fall apart when life gets tough or when there are sexual temptations. Pursuing faith together and maintaining a spiritual focus are crucial to growing a strong, close marriage.

For this reason, Kay Arthur teaches that your relationship with Christ is the glue that can bond a husband and wife together for life, the secret that can hold your marriage together.

Genesis 2:24 says when a man and a woman marry, they become one flesh. The emphasis is on physical intimacy or oneness. However, the unity the Lord wants couples to experience extends far beyond the physical dimension of the relationship. It includes intellectual and spiritual unity as well.

Humans are three-fold beings. We are physical, intellectual, and spiritual, and the Lord designed us to remain active in all three ways throughout our lives. To omit any one of these dimensions is to neglect a third of what life is all about. Some couples leave out two aspects of humanness in their marriage, focusing only on sex, disregarding the importance of the mind and the spirit. When they do this, they're ignoring two-thirds of their potential for intimacy, meaning, and happiness together. They're simply too shallow as a couple, and their marriage is headed for troubled waters, certain to crash against the rocks or run aground.

Proverbs 3:5-6 says, Trust in the Lord with all your heart, and do not rely on your own understanding; think about Him in all your ways, and He will guide you on the right paths.

The wisdom found in this proverb encourages you to acknowledge the Lord in every part of your life, including your marriage and family. In other words, if you want to know how to make your marriage work, it's important to start with making sure you are being spiritual together.

Spirituality, is a gift from God, designed to help us be our best. The Bible says every perfect gift is from above. Spirituality is a gift designed by God to help us, to bring happiness and fulfillment, to draw us closer to him, and to one another as husband and wife. It's one of the ways God empowers us, helps us make sense of the world, and make sense of our lives.

14
THE POWER OF THE TONGUE

When I came across Deborah Tannen's book, You Just Don't Understand, it looked good, so I bought it, took it home, and placed it on my nightstand. That night I picked it up and started reading, and reading, and reading. The more I read, the more I laughed out loud. The subtitle—what it's really all about—is Men and Women in Conversation.

"What are you laughing about?" my wife wondered.

"I'm laughing cause she's talking about you and me."

"What?"

Every night I read a few more pages, still laughing. I'm sure Dr. Tannen didn't mean for her book to be taken as a comedy. She wrote it as a straight-forward description of the way men and women communicate and fail to communicate, based on the way they think and their goals and purposes in the relationship. But when you see yourself and your spouse on every page, it makes you wonder, How did she know that's what we do?

How Did She Know What We Do?

I think I learned more about communication with my wife from Tannen's writing than from any other source. It was easy to see my wife's foibles and laugh about them. Aha! See? That's what you do! But then to read about what I do was a real eye-opener. I had to own up to my own patterns and behaviors.

What I learned was that Linda and I are pretty normal in how we communicate. In many ways, we fall into the stereotypes of male and female. But the way Dr. Tannen tells the stories is so funny. I called it my evening devotions. I had to read more.

One of the principles she discusses is the 3-fold asymmetry between the way men and women think and communicate.

Men talk to Report; women talk to Rapport.

When there's a problem, men move immediately into Fix-it mode; women move into Affirmation mode.

Men speak to establish Hierarchy; women speak to establish Community.

Of course, these are generalities. There are men and women at both ends of each spectrum. All too often, however, husband and wife reach a stalemate because of their differences. Not understanding their communication styles and their subconscious purposes, they become frustrated or angry with each other, and that's when they say things that hurt the other.

Proverbs 18:21 tells us that life and death are in the power of the tongue. What it's saying is we can choose the easy, angry words and slice each other to shreds, destroying each other and the marriage in the process. Or, we can carefully choose words that affirm, heal, and build each other up. When we do that, we have a fantastic opportunity to create a marriage that'll last a lifetime.

15
JACK REACHER AND MARRIAGE

Lee Child, author of the Jack Reacher novels, tells about a time when he was unemployed. While trying to begin his writing career, he got into the habit of helping his wife with chores around the house. Then, he started going to the supermarket with her to help carry the groceries. She liked this, because he was quite a bit taller, able to reach items on the top shelves. On one occasion, a little old lady asked for his help. After Lee helped the woman, his wife said, "If this writing thing doesn't work out, you can always be a reacher in a supermarket." Instantly he thought, "What a great name for my character." And Jack Reacher was born.

The irony is that he was helping her in the supermarket, and she helped him by giving him a name for the hero in his stories.

Having a proper understanding of the teaching on "help" in the Bible, couples who want their marriage to last a lifetime become extremely practical and intentional about helping their spouse in both small ways and big ways. They get good at it.

Christian psychologist Gary Smalley said helping is a powerful way of loving, empowering the partner to overcome the disasters that happen to everyone. According to Smalley, an "interest in being with and helping others during a crisis is a demonstration of love." Helping during the tough times can make or break a marriage, but having a helpful attitude and demeanor in the give and take of ordinary life is also essential.

Norman Wright and Gary Oliver point out that most couples begin their marriage responding to their partner's needs by going out of their way to meet those needs. "But in time, this changes. Where previously most of our attention was focused on our spouse's needs, our attention begins to focus on the fulfillment of our own needs. Each of us moves into the stage of giving less and expecting more." A relationship that began good, turns into disillusionment, and disillusionment invites what John Gottman calls the Four Horsemen of the Apocalypse: criticism, contempt, defensiveness, and stonewalling.

Dr. Gottman explains that once these behaviors are in the mix, the relationship is headed in the wrong direction, and may be in serious trouble. These actions simply don't help the situation, nor do they help the people involved. Talking seems useless. Husband and wife start living parallel lives. And loneliness sets in. Couples in a marriage where this is happening might feel like calling it quits. After all, that's what their friends, their families, their therapist, and the media are telling them to do. You fell in love, it didn't work out, you fell out of love. Get over it, and move on.

Throwing in the towel, however, might not be the best thing to do. That might just add more pain and failure to lives already in trouble. Instead, the wise couple will look for ways to help each other through the tough times. And, they'll look for responses that will help the marriage itself.

Marriage isn't a partnership where one is always weak and the other always strong. Everyone has strengths and weaknesses. The idea is to help each other maximize strengths, and overcome weaknesses.

When couples begin to understand that the primary role in marriage is to be a helper, they realize in a very real way that they represent God to each other. The Lord is our helper, and he places husband and wife in the marriage to act on his behalf.

The bottom line is that a husband and wife who will routinely help one another in practical ways day after day will establish a friendship and an atmosphere of love that is contagious, and noticeable to everyone who knows them. They're on their way to creating unity and developing a marriage that will last a lifetime.

16
THE UKRAINIAN OFFICER

My first Sunday at the FOB in Iraq was Palm Sunday, one week before Easter 2007. Eight people showed up for church that morning: a civilian I called Pastor James, four American soldiers who had been meeting with him faithfully for the past year, my Chaplain Assistant, one new guy, and me. It was easy to see that the soldiers respected James. He had been there for them, and they loved him. My sermon was based on Mark chapter eleven, "Blessed is he who comes in the name of the Lord." We finished worship having communion together, Pastor James and me side-by-side.

After I thanked everyone for coming and was about to dismiss the small group, a stranger in a Ukrainian army uniform walked into the chapel unannounced and proclaimed, "I have something to say."

He had an excellent command of English

vocabulary, but with a heavy accent. He was an attractive, friendly man, about 6' 2" with short hair, heavy eyebrows, and green eyes.

"I am not a Christian. Several months ago, I started having problems with my eyes. I went to the doctors here in our medical clinic. They told me I had an incurable eye condition. They brought in a specialist who confirmed the diagnosis. He said there was nothing they could do for me. No treatment. No medicine. No surgery. He said my eyes would gradually get worse until I was totally blind. Last Sunday I came here and asked the men if they would pray for me." He pointed to James and said, "That man put his hands on my head and prayed. These other guys put their hands on me and prayed too."

"The next day, last Monday, I could see better, so I went back to the clinic. The doctors did the same tests all over again. This time, they said I don't have that disease. I have been back to the clinic to see the doctors almost every day this week. Your God healed me. I am not going to lose my eyes. I am so happy. How can I become a Christian?"

You could hear the sounds of surprise and amazement from the small congregation, especially from Pastor James and the men who had prayed with him the previous Sunday. In simple terms, I explained who Jesus was and what it meant to receive him as Lord and Savior.

I wasn't a part of the miracle of healing that he experienced the previous week. Pastor James and the others had prayed for him. But on my first Sunday at Camp Echo, I had the privilege of praying with this man, a captain in the Ukrainian army, as he asked Jesus to come into his heart. The feeling among our little group was incredible.

The Ukrainian brother came alive. Every time I saw him, whether walking down the street, sitting in the DFAC, or attending a staff meeting, he hugged me, told me how thankful he was that Jesus healed him and saved him. And then he'd say, "We have to tell people about Jesus. They have to know him."

17
MY FIERY FURNACE

When they told me where I was going, they said it was the Safest Place in Iraq, but by the time I got there, things had changed. On a Tuesday night, the dining facility was crowded, bustling, with hardly an empty chair, when mortars landed on the building. Of the more than two hundred people in the dining facility, eighteen were killed. Forty-seven were wounded, some seriously, but they'd survive – with or without that arm or leg or eye.

People were stunned, walking around like zombies. Most avoided eating in the DFAC, even after it was repaired and they started serving meals again. From that moment, incoming mortars and rockets became part of the routine that was soon to be my daily life.

Located on the main rail line between Baghdad and Basra, Diwaniyah is known for its manufacturing, and famous for its automobile tires.

Dust-colored high-rise apartment buildings line the streets, each building home to more than a thousand people. Water from the Euphrates River irrigates the farms and groves outside the city, making the region one of the nation's most fertile.

Men from Diwaniyah would drive to a vacant field on the edge of town, bringing their rockets and mortars to fire at us. They did this in the morning on their way to work. Sometimes it was mid-day during a lunch break, and other times in the evening on their way home from work. Occasionally it was in the middle of the night. Some of the people shooting at us were teens or even younger. Often, they would launch their missiles-of-death just before, or right after their prayers.

Camp Echo was a small, roundish Forward Operating Base, about a mile in diameter, in the middle of the desert, with temperatures ranging from 110-120 degrees. The dirt, sand, and heat were inescapable. Every day began with a new film of dust on each desk, table, chair, bed, and floor. The layer of dirt thickened as the day wore on.

Surrounding the entire FOB was a 12-foot high concrete wall. The other side of the barrier consisted of dry fields inhabited by rabbits, snakes, and camel spiders. There were also scorpions, an occasional wild dog, and, of course, the men and boys trying to kill us.

I volunteered to go. My philosophy as an Army chaplain was that I wanted to be wherever soldiers had to go, and if they were at war, I wanted to be there with them. Not because I enjoy fighting. We all know that a chaplain is a non-combatant. I wasn't there to fight.

I was there to encourage, counsel, and pray; provide worship opportunities, friendship, and guidance; nurture the living, care for the wounded, and honor the dead; and guarantee the constitutional freedom of worship to men and women of all faiths, and the same freedom to men and women of no faith. Camp Echo was my home, my parish, my fiery furnace.

18
THE RISK OF FAITH

Daniel was thrown into a lion's den because he prayed three times a day to his God. But the Lord protected him, and the ferocious beasts lay down and purred.

Not far from there, Shadrach, Meshach, and Abed-Nego were thrown into a blazing fire because they refused to bow down and worship a golden statue. Instead, they declared,

"Our God whom we serve is able to deliver us from the fiery furnace, and He will deliver us from your hand, O king. But if not, let it be known to you, O king, that we do not serve your gods, nor will we worship the gold image which you have set up." (Daniel 3:17-18 NKJV)

Their faith didn't depend on whether they escaped. They were fully prepared to risk everything, which meant they didn't serve the Lord only during the good times. They didn't trust God only to get their way. There was nothing selfish about their prayer, their life, or their religion. Their faith in God was genuine, even when it resulted in persecution. Even when it meant risking their lives. Death was certain, and they knew it—unless God did a miracle. Either way, they were determined to be faithful.

The fire was so hot that the soldiers escorting them to the flames died on the spot. But for Shadrach, Meshach, and Abed-Nego, not a hair on their head or their arms was singed, and not a thread of their clothing burned. They never even felt the heat. It was like they were taking a walk in the park on a cool, breezy day.

When the smoke cleared, King Nebuchadnezzar looked into the furnace, and to his amazement, there was a fourth man in the flames with them. The king couldn't believe his eyes. Daniel 3:25 reports Nebuchadnezzar's amazement.

"Look! I see four men walking around in the fire, unbound and unharmed, and the fourth looks like a son of the gods." (Daniel 3:25 NIV)

Daniel understood the dangers of breaking the law and praying to his God. Hungry lions can easily tear a man apart. Shadrach, Meshach, and Abed-Nego knew the risks when they decided not to bow to the king's statue.

However, God intervened, and Daniel survived to tell the King once more about the goodness and reality of the true God. Shadrach, Meshach, and Abed-Nego, encountered the Lord right there in the middle of the blazing heat.

The eleventh chapter of Hebrews makes it clear that not everyone who takes the risk of faith will escape pain or death. I would encourage you to read the entire chapter, but verses 32–38 show how the situations turned out for some of God's people. And verse 39 adds,

"These were all commended for their faith." (Hebrews 11:39 NIV)

Being a disciple of Jesus Christ always involves risk. Some will face ridicule. Others might lose their jobs. Some are abandoned by their family. Others experience physical torture. Some will survive. Others may die. What is God asking you to risk?

The bottom line is that your faith will cost you something. God is calling you to accept the challenge, count the cost, and take the risk.

Christians in many places around the world are experiencing persecution at this moment. In the same way, it might cost you something to follow Jesus. But like those men in the book of Daniel, you can be faithful regardless of the outcome, because the fourth man in the fire is going to be there with you.

19
UNITY PRODUCES WINNERS

Football season is in full swing. All across the nation, players and fans have high hopes and great expectations that their team will win. And let's be honest, for most people, it's not how you play the game. It's whether you win or lose.

Last week, several sportswriters interviewed a college quarterback whose team just won a big game. They had beaten a good team by a pretty wide margin, and when asked how he did it, the QB deflected the praise. "It was my guys. They played a great game. I know I can count on them to come through." Another question elicited this answer, "The reason we're doing so well is that we all bought into what the coaches are telling us. There's no fighting or working against each other here."

Winners always have one thing in common: They have team chemistry and camaraderie. After a successful game, and especially after the season ends and they win the championship, a reporter inevitably asks the question, "What's special about this team? What made it possible to win it all?" And the answer is always, "We're a family. On and off the field. We have a sense of togetherness that really made it happen. I love these guys."

The same happens in any sport. Unity produces winners, and this dynamic is at play in every field, whether a business, a school, a club, a fraternity, a church, a military unit, a marriage, or a family. Even in politics.

In Matthew 12:25 Jesus says, "Every kingdom divided against itself will be ruined, and every city or household divided against itself will not stand."

A kingdom? A city? A household? The context of his statement is the spiritual realm, which means the same principles are at work in the spiritual dimension as they are in human relationships, athletics, and the business world.

We see this again in Matthew 18:19-20. "If two of you on earth agree about any matter that you pray for, it will be done for you by My Father in heaven. For where two or three are gathered together in My name, I am there among them."

According to these verses, unity turns on the power of God, and invites the presence of God. No wonder unity produces winners. We need the power and the presence of God at work in our lives and our relationships.

Years ago, my wife and I adopted the slogan "We're on the Same Team." We're both competitive, and there's a potential for one of us to feel good for winning, at the expense of the other feeling bad for losing, and we don't want that to happen. In reality, husband and wife both win, or they both lose. Everyone in the church wins, or the church loses. Just like on the football team, everyone wins, or everyone loses.

Unity produces winners.

20
WHEN THE SHIP SINKS

Fifty-five minutes past midnight on February 3, 1943 the USS Dorchester was on its way to Greenland with more than nine hundred men on board. Captain Hans Danielsen, aware that German U-boats were in the area, had ordered the men to stay ready and keep their life jackets on, but many of them disobeyed the order because the life jackets were uncomfortable and impossible to sleep in.

Four Army chaplains were on the ship: a Methodist minister, a Jewish rabbi, a Catholic priest, and a Reformed Church pastor. All four had been Boy Scouts. All four were brand new lieutenants in the Army. All four were ready to serve their Soldiers, their country, and their God. All four were prepared to give their lives if necessary.

When the torpedo hit the ship, the lights went out. A lot of people died instantly; more died in the water. Others were injured. Men who were trapped below began to panic, looking for their life jacket, trying to find a way to the top deck so they could abandon ship.

As soon as the chaos began, the four chaplains sprang into action. They encouraged panic-stricken young men, guided Soldiers towards the upper deck and to the lifeboats, and helped them find life jackets. When there were no more life preservers to be found, they took off their own and gave them away in order to save the lives of a few more men, knowing that it certainly meant they themselves would die.

Two hundred thirty men made it into the rescue boats that night. As they looked back at the sinking ship, they saw the four chaplains standing on deck, arms linked, praying and singing in Hebrew, Latin, and English.

What do you do when your ship sinks? How do you respond when your world is at its darkest and there seems to be no way of escape? Or when the future holds no promise and there seems to be no hope?

If Ecclesiastes 3:1 is true and there is an appropriate time and season for every purpose under heaven, and if different times and seasons call for different actions, then how we live, how we behave, what is appropriate, or what is best, may be more a matter of discernment than following rules. There is a time to shout and a time to whisper, a time to drop the bomb and a time to lay down the weapon, a time to wear the life jacket, and a time to give it away so another may live.

An immoral man behaves inappropriately for selfish reasons. A moral man does what is right because of legal, humanitarian, or religious obligations. A hero rejects selfishness, takes his moral obligations into account, then discerns with artistic altruism a course of action that will benefit another human being, even when that act may bring harm to himself. That's what love does. That's what genuine spirituality aims for. That's what Jesus had in mind when he said, "There is no greater love than to lay down one's life for one's friends" (John 15:13).

Most societies pay tribute to their heroes, and the four chaplains of the Dorchester are heroes who deserve that honor. They could have lived longer, ministering for many more years, making a difference, perhaps for thousands of people. Yet, discerning the time and the season, they chose to whisper, "I love you." They decided to take off their life jackets. "Here, take mine." They loved the men they ministered to, knowing it certainly meant they would die, and in making that decision, they painted a magnificent work of art.

21
HE'S NA HEAVY; HE'S MI BRITHER

Walking along a country road, a little girl struggles under the weight of a heavy load. A passerby stops to see if she needs help, and notices that she's carrying a rather large baby boy, not much smaller than herself, it seems.

"Don't you get tired carrying him?"

The little girl matter-of-factly replies, "He's na heavy; he's mi brither."

The story first appeared in Scotland in 1884, in a book on the Parables of Jesus. It showed up in the September 1924 Kiwanis magazine. Then in 1941, Father Edward Flanagan discovered a similar story with a picture in Ideal Magazine, and got permission to use the motto and image at Boys Town, the home for boys he founded.

The movie Boys Town came out in 1938. A 1941 sequel, titled The Men of Boys Town, included the line, "He ain't heavy, he's my brother." In 1969, Bob

Russell and Bobby Scott wrote a song by the same name. It became popular and was sung by dozens of pop singers in the 60s and 70s. In addition, there have been numerous paintings and sculptures on the same theme. Click on the record below and you can hear the song.

There's something about the story of the little girl that captivates the imagination and begs to illustrate a key theme in the Bible. In Genesis 4:9, the Lord asks Cain about Abel, and the murderer replies, "Am I my brother's keeper?" The answer implied in the scripture is simple. "Yes, you are your brother's keeper." Leviticus 19:18 instructs the people of God to "Love your neighbor as yourself," which Jesus quotes in Matthew 22:37. The apostle Paul adds in Galatians 6:2 that we are to "Carry one another's heavy load, and by doing so, fulfill the law of Christ."

In Victor Hugo's timeless novel, Les Misérable, Jean Valjean is a former criminal who changes his name and his lifestyle in order to hide his past, eventually becoming the mayor of a town. But the new chief of police is the very same officer who was a guard at the prison, and is looking to re-arrest Valjean for breaking parole. One day, one of the men in town is trapped under the heavy weight of a horse-drawn wagon, and nobody is able to get him out from underneath. Then, while Javert, the police inspector, is watching, the mayor hefts the weight of the wagon, lifting it off the ground high enough for others to pull the man to safety.

The officer remembers a time when a prisoner had done something similar in the prison, and wonders if this is the same man. Knowing what's at stake, Valjean risks his identity and his freedom in order to help the man.

Carrying one another's burden is the essence of loving someone in the name of the Lord, loving someone enough to lighten the load, loving someone enough to risk everything in order to offer a helping hand.

The Parable of the Good Samaritan in Luke chapter 10 has a similar motif. In this story, several righteous people see the injured man, but they don't stop to help him. The one who provides the desperately needed assistance is an outsider, a despised Samaritan, someone you'd least expect to offer help. But he does stop, and he does help. In fact, he pays the innkeeper to care for the man until he returns.

After telling the story, Jesus asks, "Which of these three do you think was a neighbor to the man who fell into the hands of robbers?" An expert in the law replies, "The one who had mercy on him." Jesus tells him, "Go and do likewise."

It is this Go and Do Likewise that Jesus asks his followers to put into practice. Are we big enough to see every human being as our neighbor, and every person out there as a brother or sister? To put it into the words of the little Scottish girl, "He's na heavy; he's mi brither."

22
HEAT, DANGER, DUST, AND DEATH

I knew from the start of my military service in Iraq that I could be wounded or killed. It was a weird feeling, and I came to accept it. How or when, I had no idea. But every time there was another explosion, I wondered if this was the day.

My wife also knew I might not make it home alive. Or if I did return, I might be a broken man – crippled, blind, psychologically damaged, or all of the above. With that possibility in mind, she told me before I left home, "I don't want to find out after you get back or after you're dead that you were in danger. I want to know right away."

Many of our military personnel won't tell their spouse and family what they're going through during war, thinking they're protecting them. Plus, we're limited in what we're allowed to say or write to our families. But I have a hunch there are many, like my wife, who are better off knowing what's going on, and who want to know.

The first time I mentioned during a phone call some of the dangerous things that were happening, she said, "I already know. I saw it on TV and in the newspaper. They're mentioning Diwaniyah and Camp Echo by name." She scanned and sent me an LA Times article. I took it to our staff meeting the next morning, and discovered that many on our leadership team didn't know what was going on outside the wire.

Heat, danger, dust, and death formed the context for the job I was sent to do. Operating from the philosophy that "ministry follows friendship," I built relationships among the men and women at Camp Echo: military, civilian, American, and Coalition. This allowed me to be there when they were at their best and when they were at their worst, in their strongest moments and in their weakest.

In the heat of the battle and the heat of the desert, hours turn into days, which transition to nights, and add up to weeks and then months. The conditions wear you down, leaving an imprint on your mind and your soul: images that will be seen in dreams for months or years, sounds that reverberate long after you're home, people you befriended and cared about and stared at death with, but will probably never hear from again. For many of us, it's only memory now. But for others, the war continues on the inside.

23
IN A HURRY AND RUNNING LATE

As a newlywed attending a Christian college in Southern California, I was a driver for a private mail and parcel service. Every day, I was in posh high-rise office buildings and run-down strip malls, machine shops and Mom-and-Pop shops. By the time I worked there a year, I'd been in almost every post office in Orange County.

One day my boss asked me to come in early because we had a new corporate client in Newport Beach who requested an early pick-up and delivery. Before heading out, I checked my map. Traffic was heavy. I was in a hurry and running late.

When I got to the post office, I turned into the drive, only to discover that I was in a long, narrow, one-way exit lane with a big red sign announcing DO NOT ENTER. The situation demanded a fast decision. Do I back up into traffic and go around the block, looking for the entrance? Or do I step on the gas and zip into the parking lot before any one tries to exit? I pressed the pedal to the metal.

When I was almost out of the wrong-way lane, a car turned into the driveway. We both slammed on the brakes, barely avoiding a head-on collision. A bit shaken by the near-miss, I pulled up to the loading dock and put my mail onto a cart, but before I walked into the rear door of the post office, that same car sped around the building and screeched to a halt. Dressed in an expensive business suit, the driver got out and stomped towards me.

Instantly, Matthew 5:25 came to mind, "Make peace with your adversary while you're still on your way."

As the stranger approached, I walked up to him and said. "Sir, I owe you an apology. In a hurry, I drove into the exit. I was wrong, and would like to ask for your forgiveness."

"Do you know who I am?" he demanded.

"No, sir. I just know that what I did was wrong. I nearly caused an accident, and I am sorry."

"I am the postmaster," his face a deep red by now. "I could ban you from every post office in the county. I could have the police ticket you for driving the wrong way. I could call your boss and have you fired." When he paused, we stared nose to nose. "But tell you what. Because you admitted your wrongdoing without even knowing who I was, I will forgive you. Don't let it happen again."

I stood there stunned. If the Holy Spirit didn't bring that verse to my mind at that instant, I would be in big trouble. If I let pride keep me from admitting my mistake, I might be unemployed by the end of the day.

It dawned on me that I really can trust the scripture when it says, "don't worry about how to defend yourself, for the Holy Spirit will tell you what to say" Matthew 10:19-20. I had memorized those verses long before that morning, never realizing that I'd need to use them in a tight situation. Before driving away, I took a minute to thank the Lord for his Word and his Spirit.

After completing my route, I parked the van and took the keys to the office. While I filled out the time sheet, my boss walked in and said, "Hey, just wanted to let you know that the Newport Beach postmaster called to tell me he met you this morning."

I froze.

"He said he was really impressed with you, and that you do good work. I Just wanted to pass that compliment on. Good job."

Embarrassed, humbled, and relieved, I drove to the college. I was in a hurry and running late, barely getting there in time for class, but careful to obey every traffic sign.

24
E-5 FOR LIFE

When I was in Iraq, I showed up at the dining facility later than usual one day. I had spent a lot of time in the medical clinic that day, and also with two units who'd lost some Soldiers. I was tired and hungry, and finding an empty seat was difficult because several visiting units were at our FOB to assist with the war, and many of the Soldiers were in the DFAC.

I finally found an empty chair and placed my tray on the table. But, before I had a chance to sit down, a Master Sergeant next to the empty seat growled in my direction, "No officers welcome here."

Obviously, the guy couldn't keep me from sitting there. He had no authority here, and clearly, I outranked him. I doubt that he noticed the cross on my uniform. He probably just saw the Major insignia on my chest, but it might not have made a difference even if he had recognized that I was a chaplain.

A lot of NCO's and officers don't like each other; don't respect each other. It's like there's an invisible barrier keeping us apart. But this guy had an aggressive attitude. Maybe because of the war; maybe because of something that happened in the past. There were three possible Courses of Action, and I had to make a quick decision.

COA #1: Look for a different chair

COA #2: Attempt to pull rank

COA #3: Tell him I am an Honorary NCO

After completing a really quick SWOT analysis, I came to attention, turned up my collar to reveal a Sergeant's E-5 insignia, and shouted as loud as I could, "Request permission to sit at your table, Master Sergeant," then remained standing at attention and waited.

The growler did a double-take, and his eyes got real big. "Have a seat, Sarge."

The other NCO's at the table were howling with laughter by now. They knew the Master Sergeant, but they didn't know me. And they had never seen a Major with NCO rank under the collar. They found the whole encounter to be quite entertaining.

After the others at the table calmed down, the slightly embarrassed and flabbergasted Master Sergeant said, "OK. S'pose you tell me why you're wearing that rank."

"Sure, Master Sergeant. When I was a rookie chaplain fresh out of Officer Basic, my first assignment was with a medical unit, where I had a great rapport with the NCO's. When they invited me to their "Dining In" at the end of the year, I thought it was because they wanted me to do the invocation, but that wasn't it. During the program, the First Sergeant pinned the NCO insignia on me, gave me a certificate, and appointed me to the honorary rank of Sergeant, making me an E-5 for Life."

"Hmmm. And you actually wear it?"

"Yes."

I wore the SGT Stripes invisibly throughout my career. When in the woodland Battle Dress Uniform, it was pinned under my collar. When we switched to the Army Combat Uniform, it was velcroed under the collar. And when I wore the Class A uniform or the Dress Blues, it was under the pocket flap, beneath my name. Every time I went to a new unit, I met with the First Sergeant or Sergeant Major, presented the documentation, and asked for permission to wear the rank and be part of the NCO corps. I was always welcomed.

Those Sergeant stripes were under the collar when I went outside the wire with the MiTT team. They accompanied me every time I visited wounded Soldiers at the medical clinic. I wore them at each memorial ceremony or funeral. They were there for the worship services, the counseling appointments, and the Critical Incident Stress Management sessions. Whenever we had incoming rockets or mortars and we gathered in the bunkers . . . yep, still had them with me.

One time, I was eating lunch when sirens started blaring. In a hurry to get out to the bunker, I forgot my helmet. My chaplain assistant grabbed me by the collar and pulled me back inside, "Chaplain, you forgot your Kevlar!" Just then. A mortar landed right outside the door. It's quite possible that she saved my life or prevented injury. See why O love NCO's?

The day after I met the Master Sergeant in the DFAC, he showed up in my office. The night before, he was feisty and energetic; now he seemed sad and tired. Something had happened.

"Good afternoon, Master Sergeant. What can I do for you?"

"This morning, I lost a Soldier ... a close friend. I wanted to know if you'd do a memorial ceremony tomorrow morning before we head out."

"Of course, I will."

"And Chaps, I'm sorry about last night."

"Not a problem, Master Sergeant. I understand."

"You can sit at my table any time."

It meant a lot that this senior NCO welcomed me at his table, that he wanted me to be there to honor his friend, and that we had overcome the invisible barrier between officer and NCO.

In 2015 I retired I retired from the military as a Colonel. But I'll be an E-5 for life.

25
METAMORPHOSIS

Butterflies are special to me for several reasons. First is the fact that they represent the internal and external changes that take place when a person comes to faith in Jesus Christ. Second is the mystery, or as some writers call it, the "magic" of the changes that occur during the transformation process. Third is the gorgeous coloration of so many species. They are delightful to find and examine.

Romans 12:2 indicates that we are to be transformed by the renewing of the mind. The word in the Greek text is where we get the English word metamorphosis. Translated as transformed, it is what we use to describe the continuous, remarkable change of form or structure in an individual after hatching or birth.

Several insects undergo complete metamorphosis, such as bees, ants, ladybugs, wasps, and flies. But the most spectacular of the metamorphosing creatures are the butterflies. This is because they are safe, easy to observe, and they are beautiful. These marvelous creatures are called Lepidoptera, which means scaly wings.

Amazingly, transformation occurs in every stage of the butterfly's life. There is never a day when an egg, caterpillar, chrysalis, or butterfly is the same as it was the day before. Theirs is literally a continuous transformation. This is also true of people. We are always growing, changing, and becoming. There's always more to learn, and always room for refinement.

26
MAN OF THE HOUSE

The phone rang on a Saturday afternoon.
"Hello," I answered.
"Hello, I'd like to speak to the man of the house."
"We don't have one," I stated matter-of-factly.

The caller didn't know what to say, so after a few seconds, I hung up.

Please understand. I am a man. The only man who lives in our house, by the way. Our three sons are grown and have homes of their own, so technically, I am "the" man of "the" house. But that's not what the caller meant.

He wanted to talk to the person who had authority to make decisions, the person who didn't have to check with someone else before spending a lot of money, the person who was in charge. And he assumed, as many do, that a woman can't make decisions, can't spend without permission, and can't be in charge.

That demeaning, unbiblical view of women and marriage is what I objected to, and that is the kind of skewed gender-role relationship that we don't have in our home.

I spoke with another caller, and what he was selling actually sounded like a good deal. But when he got to the point where he wanted to close the sale, I mentioned that I wasn't going to make a decision on the spot, because I wanted to discuss it with my wife. I couldn't believe his sarcastic response. "What's the matter? Aren't you the man of the house? Can't you make a decision?"

I'm not sure what he thought when I said, "My wife and I respect each other enough to talk about major expenses, and we make shared decisions. So, go ahead and call someone else, someone who doesn't understand how to build a good marriage, and try to bully him instead."

The fact is, my wife and I both make decisions; we're pretty good at it, too. We trust each other and support each other. We're not perfect by any means, but our usual practice is to take time to talk together before making major decisions. It's one of the ways we've been able to maintain unity. We value one another and what each other thinks and feels. It's also a matter of courtesy.

According to Dr. Gary Chapman, very few decisions have to be made today. Unity is more important than haste. In other words, a good decision at the expense of unity is a bad decision.

27
A TURKISH PROVERB

In 2008, developers built some high-rise condos on the South Texas Coast. Ocean Tower was supposed to provide luxurious amenities and beautiful views, but it didn't take long for the entire structure to begin to sink, and then tilt, with wide cracks in the concrete support system.

According to an old Turkish proverb, "A building without a foundation is soon demolished." The foundation wasn't prepared well enough, and the whole project had to be destroyed after more than seventy-five million dollars had been invested.

The famous, leaning bell tower in Pisa, Italy, on the other hand, stood straight for five years before the 14,500-ton structure began to sink. It managed to survive, but as we all know, there is a serious slant.

In Matthew chapter seven, Jesus talks about the importance of a foundation for a home. But, just like in Proverbs 24:3-4, what he's really talking about is people, and in this case, the need for an inner, spiritual foundation.

Couples who want their marriage to survive storms and shifting sands, need to make sure they have a foundation that will last a lifetime.

Several years ago, my wife and I did a short-term missions trip to Budapest, Hungary, teaching a three-week intensive class at the Hungarian Bible college, and preaching at churches in and around the city. Our hosts were a missionary family that allowed us to stay in an upstairs bedroom in their home.

Looking out a second-story window, we noticed the neighbors were building another home on their property, immediately behind the main house. The missionaries explained that it was customary for children to grow up and live on the same property as their parents. The new building was for their son, who was about to get married. The foundation was already in place, and every day, we came back to the house, looked out the window, and followed the progress. We watched the walls grow higher as new rows of bricks were added.

God's plan for marriage is vastly different from the typical concept of marriage in the world today. Rather than a battle zone, marriage is designed to be peaceful. Rather than causing you pain, it can be a source of profound healing. Rather than a selfish coexistence, a good marriage is a loving couple coming together to help and encourage one another. Rather than a ball and chain, marriage liberates you to reach your goals and see your dreams come true. Rather than a hell, marriage can be a heaven on earth. And, rather than a temporary arrangement, marriage is best when it takes you through all phases of life . . . together. For that to happen, however, the relationship has to be built on a solid foundation.

28
THE OLD CHEVY

When we drove up to the historic motel on Route 66, an old Chevy parked out front caught our eye. It had to be more than sixty-five years old, and though the paint was faded, worn-off, and rust-eaten the car still exuded a certain charm and beauty. A couple of the tires were flat and one window was permanently open. Yet, it had a stately dignity that spoke of a time when it ruled the road.

Once upon a time, this automobile was the lifeline for an entire family. Dad drove it to work; Mom took it shopping. Weekends were for family outings, and Sundays for going to Church. Each summer she took her family to a far-off destination, and special occasions saw her at family get-togethers. The kids learned to drive behind that huge steering wheel, and longed for the day they might get a car of their own: something new, shiny, and fast, with the latest technology.

But the old Chevy had long ago been discarded. Removed to the junkyard, where it sat for a decade: unwanted, untended, and ignored. Just taking up space.

Sometimes we look at people that way. We have no time for the elderly, no interest in what they have to offer or what they've accomplished. They had their day in the sun; now it's our turn. We look at people of different ethnicities similarly. We too easily disregard their importance, their feelings, their dreams and ambitions, and what they can contribute to the community or the church. We treat children as though they were worth less than adults, and teens as if they should be banished to a remote island.

The Bible, on the other hand, tells us to honor people, value them, and care for them. To look for the beauty and the charm that are still there in every human being. Romans 12:10, for example, says to honor and give preference to one another.

James 1:27 reminds us that "pure and undefiled religion in the sight of our God and Father is this: to look after orphans and widows in their affliction." In other words, we're supposed to honor those in society who are helpless or in less fortunate circumstances.

The writer of Job adds to this discussion by recognizing the dignity of the common person and by identifying with the hireling and the slave. "Do not mortals have hard service on earth? Are not their days like those of hired laborers? Like a slave longing for the evening shadows, or a hired laborer waiting to be paid?"

In context, Job is saying there's no difference between the rich and the poor, the master and the slave, when it comes to how hard life can be. We all want rest at the end of the day, we all want a better life for our family, we all have hopes and dreams, we all need love and friendship, and we all crave acceptance and respect.

The apostle Paul summarizes in Philippians chapter two, where he simply says we are to value others above ourselves.

The woman who owned the roadside hotel told us that a lot of her customers express an interest in old cars and the way life used to be on Route 66. So, she called a friend who had a junkyard, and asked if there was an old car she could buy. Her friend gave her the Chevy and brought it to her motel, where it has attracted attention and sparked conversation among people from all over the country and all around the world who see the car while driving by.

29
YADA, YADA, YADA

The April 24, 1997 episode of the Seinfeld Show was titled *the Yada, Yada*. Neither Jerry Seinfeld nor the show's writers coined the phrase "yada, yada." It was already in use. But after being included on the show, the expression skyrocketed in popularity and is still used by a lot of people.

There's some debate about the origin of the phrase. Some say it's from the English expression yatter, while others say it comes from the Norwegian jada, which is pronounced the same and means the same as yada. Other sources say it comes from Yiddish or Hebrew. In any case, it usually means the same as blah, blah, blah, or et cetera, et cetera, et cetera. Instead of reciting the boring details of a story, you say "yada, yada, yada" instead.

When you watch *the Yada, Yada* episode, however, it's quite obvious from the way the characters tell their stories that there's a sexual connotation and an intentional double meaning going on. Apparently, there is some evidence that *yada* is, indeed, a euphemism for sex. If so, when the Seinfeld cast says "yada, yada, yada" in those stories, what they're really saying is "sex, sex, sex." Watch it on YouTube and see if it seems that way to you.

Because people are sometimes shy about discussing sex, we often use euphemisms when talking about it. Some of those expressions are making love, going all the way, doing it, hanky-panky, and hitting a home run. My sister and her husband use the phrase "twice around the park" when referring to sex. My wife and I use a different term.

Our teen-aged son never wanted to talk when we wanted to; he always waited 'til late at night. When we were way past ready to go to bed . . . that's when he was just coming alive and wanted to talk. One night he asked, "Hey guys. Wha'd you do on your honeymoon?" I have no idea what brought that question to his mind, or what he expected us to say.

There's a lot of things we did on our honeymoon, but the one that came to mind was, "Well, Son. We played backgammon. Someone gave us a backgammon game as a wedding gift, and we took it with us. We stopped at a store, bought some instructions, and learned to play the game while on our honeymoon."

"Oh. Okay." Apparently, that satisfied his curiosity for the time being.

Two weeks later, we were in our bedroom with the door closed, but still fully clothed, playing backgammon on the bed, when there was a knock on the bedroom door. Same son wanted to talk.

"Dad, can we talk about something?"

"Sure, Son. Come on in."

When he opened the door and saw us on the bed, his jaw dropped, eyes opened wide. "Oh my gosh! You really do play backgammon!"

"What did you think I meant?"

"Uh . . . I thought you made it up 'cause you didn't want to talk about what you really did on your honeymoon!"

"Oh! Well, we really did play backgammon."

"Oh. My. Gosh."

Ever since that conversation, "backgammon" has been a euphemism for sex in our family. "So that's what you did on your honeymoon, heh heh."

Yada = Knowing

When Genesis 4:1 says Adam was intimate with his wife Eve, the word translated as intimate is the Hebrew word *yada*. The Hebrew Bible, called the Tanach, from the Jewish Publication Society translates this verse, "Now the man knew his wife Eve, and she conceived and bore Cain." The word "knew" has a footnote that says, "Heb. yada, often in a sexual sense." Following the Jewish understanding of *yada* in this context, many English translations of Genesis 4:1 keep the idea to know.

The word means "to know intimately, to know completely, to be familiar." No wonder one of its additional meanings is to know sexually.

Other translations render the verse as follows. These are all appropriate ways to translate Genesis 4:1, where it says in Hebrew, Adam yada'd his wife.

Adam and Eve had a son.
The man knew his wife.
Adam had sexual intercourse with his wife.
Adam slept with his wife.
Adam had relations with his wife.
Adam made love to his wife.

One of John Gottman's *Seven Principles for Making Marriage Work* is what he calls "Love Maps." Couples with a strong, resilient marriage not only know each other, they know a lot about each other. "From knowledge springs not only love but the fortitude to weather marital storms. Couples who have detailed love maps of each other's world are far better equipped to cope with stressful events and conflict."

I met Dr. Gottman when he spoke at a college in Orlando a few years ago. During a private conversation about love maps, he said it's not an accident that the word "know" is used for sexual intimacy in Genesis 4:1. Knowing each other is crucial to maintaining a satisfying love life.

30
LIGHT OF THE WORLD

When the queen of England knighted Sir Isaac Newton, it was the first time a scientist was honored this way. He was a brilliant scholar with a wide range of interests: from mathematics to natural philosophy, from the laws of motion to the laws of gravity, from the study of optics to the study of theology.

His first series of lectures at Trinity College, Cambridge, was on optics. Other scientists had begun the scientific revolution, and the study of light was a central theme. Newton made significant contributions to the scientific understanding of white light and color. He even built the first reflecting telescope.

Light is a fascinating topic, and because of its significance, Jesus used it as a metaphor for himself when he made the statement in John 8:12, "I AM the light of the world." There are at least five reasons why light is important, and these factors provide insight as to what the Lord was saying.

First, light is essential for vision. Have you ever noticed as the sun goes down late in the day, shadows grow darker, and it's more difficult to see? If the moon and the stars aren't in the night sky, by the time it's pitch black you see nothing.

Light is also essential for color. As the light dims, colors fade. For this reason, light is a necessary ingredient for beauty in the world.

Third, the earth's food chain depends on light. Photosynthesis is the process whereby plants use the energy of light to produce food. In other words, without light, there is no life.

It's also worth noting that for a lot of people, light is a key element of happiness. Many studies have shown higher levels of depression where there is less natural light. This seems to be true for some who work indoors, as well as for those who live in areas where there are seasonally shorter days.

One more observation is that light can drive away fear. When our son was five years old, we'd put him to bed at night, singing a song and praying with him before turning out the light. In a few minutes, we'd hear him yelling, "There's a wolf!"

"No, son. There's not a wolf."

"Yes, there is. Would you leave the light on?"

When the light was on, he could see, so he wasn't afraid. But in the dark, his imagination slipped into high gear, and he was afraid.

The impact when Jesus comes into a person's life

is similar to light in the natural world. He opens our eyes, giving us vision. He adds color and beauty to our lives. He brings life and happiness, and drives away fear. Our Creator already knew what Sir Isaac Newton and other scientists took years to figure out, because he created light.

In Matthew 5:14, he who is the Light of the World turns to his disciples and in a stunning plot twist tells them, and us, "You are the light of the world." We are called to be Christ to our world. The effect of our interacting with people and the planet should add vision, beauty, life, and happiness. And, wherever there's a Christian presence, there should be less fear.

In the same way God sent his son into the world not to condemn, but to save, he sends us into the world with the same mission. When we represent the Lord the way he hopes we will, that's when the church is at its best, becomes most productive, remains relevant, and changes the world.

31
ARIZONA POTHOLE

The Lord must have been showing off his artistic skills when he made northern Arizona. On a cross-country trip, we visited the Painted Desert, the Petrified Forest, and the Grand Canyon. Such beauty on a massive scale.

We enjoyed downtown Flagstaff, and even spent some time standing on a corner in Winslow. Then, after a day in Kingman, we decided to drive out to the town of Oatman, on Old Route 66. We heard that the wild burros roaming the desert also walk the streets of Oatman, but we discovered they practically rule the town. In fact, they were the main attraction for many of the visitors. And, rather than being "wild," they were definitely people-friendly. Even little children were feeding and petting the animals.

Our day-trip was delayed, however, because on the way to Oatman, we hit a pothole. We weren't going very fast, but the cavity in the pavement was deep, its sharp edges instantly puncturing the tire. Our only option was to pull off to the side, call for a tow truck, and wait . . . and wait . . . and wait.

Sometimes life happens that way. We make our plans and have a schedule to keep, but suddenly something happens and we find ourselves unable to do what we wanted to do. That's when our automatic response system kicks into gear, and it's usually negative.

Some people get angry. "Great! Our day is ruined."

Some become sad or depressed. "Why did this happen to us? This is horrible."

Others start blaming. "If you were watching where you were going, this wouldn't have happened. It's all your fault."

Or criticizing. "I can't believe they'd leave a huge pothole like that. They obviously aren't doing their job."

When things don't work out the way we planned, or the way we hoped they would, it's better to remember the words of Philippians 4:12, "I have learned the secret of being content in any and every situation" (NIV). That's hard to do, but so important if we want to maintain a sense of joy and happiness.

If we can train ourselves to stay positive, and if we can discipline ourselves to avoid the automatic negative tendencies of our personalities, then hitting a pothole doesn't have to ruin our day. Nor does it have to become a point of tension in a relationship.

It could actually become a catalyst for discovering a blessing that the Lord might have in mind for us.

Can you imagine Paul and Silas sitting in prison, grumbling, blaming each other or the government, getting depressed, and complaining about the conditions in the jail? No, that's not what they did. Acts 16:25 tells us that "about midnight Paul and Silas were praying and singing" (HCSB). Their joyous faith during terrible circumstances led to the jailer's family putting their faith in Christ.

James 1:2 reminds us to "count it all joy when you fall into various trials" (NKJV), because it's often through the disappointments of life that the Lord is able to shape us, refine us, and develop our character. And sometimes, he performs a miracle or answers a prayer in the process.

The tow truck finally arrived, the driver put our car on the flatbed, and took us back to Kingman. The repair shop didn't have the tire we needed, so they had to overnight one from Phoenix. Since it wouldn't get there til the next day, we rented a car and went to Oatman to see the burros. That evening, we had an unplanned date night. Dinner and a movie in Kingman, Arizona.

32
THE CHEMISTRY OF FALLING IN LOVE

Experts researching the biology and chemistry of falling in love and falling out of love have discovered there is a 2-year cycle of attraction, that is largely hormonal and chemical. What we call falling in love is the rush of hormones and chemicals that bring an excitement, arousal, happiness, and energy. You feel so good when you're with the new lover, or even when thinking about him or her. It's intoxicating.

Then after about two years, that chemical/hormonal cocktail begins to lose its effect. You don't feel the same, and you wonder what went wrong in the relationship, why you fell out of love.

George Strait recorded a song titled I Ain't Her Cowboy Anymore about a guy whose lover is leaving, and he has no clue what he did wrong . . . or whether he did anything wrong at all.

The answer? Nothing went wrong. There's a normal cycle that's part of developing a mature relationship. Yes, it's ignited by the passion and the internal chemistry, but then you have to build your marriage on a solid foundation so when the newness wears off, you don't fall into the trap of thinking, "Oh we're not in love anymore. It's just not meant to be. Maybe I married the wrong person."

The plan is to fall madly in love, and then take the time and the effort to install the relationship values, skills, and patterns that'll take you through every phase of married life . . . Happy and together.

Let's simplify things here. There are two goals in marriage: stay together, and stay happy. Easy to say; tough to do. You need wisdom if you want to reach those goals.

Proverbs 24:3-4 says, A house is built by wisdom, and it is established by understanding; by knowledge the rooms are filled with every precious and beautiful treasure.

When the proverb uses the word house or home, it's really talking about the people and the relationships in the home. A house is built by wisdom, means developing a great relationship requires wisdom. And filling its rooms with every precious and beautiful treasure is what every couple, family, and household should be trying to do.

You've got to build your house in such a way that you discover the beauty, the grandeur, and the treasures God has for you. In the same way every home is decorated differently, no two marriages will look and feel the same. Your relationship will be unique because you are one-of-a-kind, but you can learn how to bring out the best in yourself, your partner, and your coupleness.

33
DRIVING WITH A BAD ATTITUDE

I used to drive more than fifty miles to work, and the same distance home in the evening. The traffic was usually pretty bad, often rainy, and as you've probably experienced, other drivers are sometimes not very nice. When I started despising drivers who made stupid decisions, I developed a bad attitude and realized I needed to do something about it.

After praying, I decided to come up with a phrase I could say whenever another driver irked me. Here's what I ended up with.

> You Are a Fabulous Human Being
> Fashioned in the Indelible Image of the Creator

After I memorized the sentence, I started saying it whenever a driver did something dumb or dangerous: ten, eleven, a dozen times a day. Nobody else knew what I was doing. I'm the only one who heard me, even though I said it out loud. It helped me remember that every man and every woman has the divine image, even those who are not living for the Lord. Even those who are terrible drivers.

Being in God's image and likeness is an important part of the Judeo-Christian world view. We're not merely the product of a godless evolutionary process. While we may have many similarities with the animals, what distinguishes us from the rest of creation is the image of God. The very first page of the Bible says, "God created man in His own image; male and female. God blessed them, and God said to them, "Be fruitful, multiply, fill the earth, and subdue it. Rule the fish of the sea, the birds of the sky, and every creature that crawls on the earth" (Genesis 1:27-28).

The Westminster Shorter Catechism poses the question, "How did God create man?" And then provides the answer, "God created man male and female after his own image, in knowledge, righteousness, and holiness, with dominion over the creatures."

To be in God's image has two meanings. First, it means we are like him. Second, it means we represent him.

How we are like God refers to his activity and character and the ways we are like him. God communicates. He creates. He relates. He loves. He keeps his word. He is loyal. He is compassionate. He has knowledge. We can make these same statements of human beings, because we are fashioned in his image. We have the ability to create, to communicate, to relate, and to love. We have moral capabilities such as loyalty and honesty. We have an ability to show compassion. We have the capacity for knowledge. And like our creator, we have the ability to make our world a better place.

The fact that we represent God has a different focus and a different starting point for how we think and live. The emphasis is not on how we are like God, but that we represent the Lord. We represent God and his values to the planet and to other people. We represent him in matters of social justice and spirituality, which is why Christians should be involved in the community, setting an example of alleviating pain in the world, and caring for the needy.

In 2 Corinthians 5:20 the apostle writes, "Now then, we are ambassadors for Christ." Not only do we have the divine image, we have the Holy Spirit in us, another powerful reason for understanding we are to represent the Lord at all times, even when driving on the freeway.

34
THE WISDOM OF WHALES

While visiting friends and family in San Diego, my wife and I decided to spend an afternoon at Seaport Village, one of our favorite places. After lunch, we stepped into the Wyland Gallery and saw the sculpture of a humpback whale nudging her newborn to the surface for its first breath, and we couldn't help but stop, stand, and stare. It's a breathtaking work of art, designed to show the beauty, compassion, and wisdom of a mother as she instinctively helps her baby take that first breath of life-giving fresh air.

We've seen humpback whales bubble-net feeding, emerging from under water, going up into the air to catch herring in their mouths. After that experience, we read about these school-bus-size behemoths, amazed at the wonderful work of the Lord in His creation. But to see the tenderness of this act of the loving mother caring for her young was overwhelming. And Wyland's artisanship is impressive.

The bronze sculpture of the whale and her infant reminds me of a story in First Kings chapter seven, where Solomon brought in a skilled craftsman to create bronze decorations for the temple. The scripture describes the items Huram fashioned. There were two massive pillars, interwoven chains, pomegranates, and lilies. He made an ocean, encircled by gourdes and resting on twelve bulls. Next, he crafted ten movable stands that were adorned with lions, bulls, and cherubim. He finished his work with basins, pots, shovels, and sprinkling bowls, all out of cast metal.

But what really caught my attention was the word "wisdom" in 1 Kings 7:14. The artist was skilled, knowledgeable, and had great insight. But wisdom? That's not what I expected to see in the description of the craftsman at work.

When I asked my wife about it, she mentioned that a good artist needs wisdom, not only to know how to work with the materials at hand, but to convey meaning to others. It's this type of wisdom that God had given to Huram as he built the bronze artifacts for the temple of the Lord. His artistic ability was a gift from God, further developed and refined by study, practice, and hard work, and offered back to the Lord as an act of worship.

First Corinthians 12:8 says wisdom is one of the Gifts of the Spirit. We need this gift, not only in the Church, but in our homes, our families, and our careers. Wisdom can help us handle tough situations. It will provide guidance when we're facing temptation, and insight for those difficult decisions that seem to come up too often. We need wisdom for knowing how to share Christ with our friends, how to pray for someone in need, and how best to answer questions from our children. Sometimes, a word of wisdom spoken at just the right time, can provide guidance for our church leaders or even the entire congregation.

If the Lord gives wisdom to a mother whale so she can safely guide her calf, and if He imparts wisdom to an artist or a craftsman in bronze, then we can be confident He will provide the wisdom and guidance we need for the circumstances, challenges, and opportunities in our lives.

35
REST FROM PAIN AND REST FROM WRONG

Many people experience the worst life has to offer. Sometimes, the pain is the result of illness or accident, but at times it is intentionally inflicted by other people.

Debbie grew up in a Christian home, and shortly after high school, met Kyle, a young man who attended the same church. After dating for a year, Kyle asked her to marry him, and she said "yes," expecting to live happily ever after.

A few months after the wedding, however, Debbie was still on cloud nine when something went terribly wrong. When she got home from work one day, she found out he'd been drinking, and in a rage, he hit her. Horrified, she called their pastor, who provided counseling for several weeks. Things seemed to be getting better, until one night Kyle put a loaded gun to her head. In a panic, Debbie managed to escape. Even though her grandmother lived several miles away, Debbie somehow found the strength to run all the way. She survived, but something inside had broken, making it hard to trust anyone. She left Kyle and abandoned her faith in Christ.

Every one of us is broken in some way. We might look fine on the outside, but inside we're hurting. If we're to find healing or any positive result from the pain, it might be helpful to take a look at Job, James, and Jesus to see how we can respond in painful circumstances.

Even though he did everything right, Job suffered terrible business losses, extreme physical pain, the death of his children, and undeserved accusations from his friends. His wife also lost everything, and chose to let go of hope and faith, suggesting that he do the same. Instead, Job turned to the Lord, and began to understand more fully his own weakness and need for God. These are important lessons that sometimes have to be learned the hard way. We have a tendency to be self-sufficient, unaware of our desperate need for God. In his darkest moments, Job chose to turn toward the Lord, and so can we.

The second possibility for meaning in our pain is character growth. James 1:2-4 tells us to remain joyful when we endure tests and trials, because they will help us mature. It is true that pain can break us, but it also has a way of strengthening us and deepening us. The difference is how we respond to the crisis and to the work of the Holy Spirit.

A third potential benefit of tribulation is that it can help us develop compassion for others. When Jesus looked at the crowds, he saw their need and was moved to compassion. He cared about people and saw their hurts. He felt their need, and acted. He fed them, healed them, taught them, loved them. The Apostle Paul picks up this theme in 2 Corinthians 1:4 when he says the Lord comforts us in our troubles so that we can comfort others.

Some people respond to pain by becoming hardened, bitter, or angry. Others are jealous of those who seem to have everything going right. If we want to grow in Christ and enjoy life to its fullest, however, we can't afford to let either of those happen. Instead, we can turn to the Lord, mature as human beings, and develop a sense of compassion for others.

There's a song in the musical version of Les Misérables that a Christian pastor sings to a hungry, homeless criminal, "Come in, sir, for you are weary, and the night is cold out there. There's a bed to rest til morning, rest from pain and rest from wrong."

That's what the Lord is saying to us in Matthew 11:28. "Come to me, you who are tired, carrying a heavy load, and I will give you rest." Rest from pain, and rest from wrong.

36
INVISIBLE FORCES

Rain and snow fall on the Little Belt Mountains in the Lewis and Clark National Forest, ninety miles east of Helena, sixty miles south of Great Falls. Streams and creeks flow past the towns of Neihart and Monarch, past Camp Rotary and the Logging Creek Campground, on their way to the Missouri River. But most of the water seeps deep into the soil, draining into the water table known as the Madison Aquifer, where it becomes invisible.

The Madison is a huge reservoir of fresh water, lying underneath five U.S. states and three Canadian provinces. This hidden water is moving. It's flowing. It's active. It provides water for thousands of wells, springs, and streams, and becomes the sustainer of life for countless people, animals, plants, and trees. Ponderosa Pine and Douglas Fir dominate the hillsides, providing shelter for black bear, elk, and white-tailed deer.

The aquifer's underground consists of layered limestone, which allows some of the water to trickle through until it finds its way to Giant Springs, outside the city of Great Falls. Once the water gets there, hydraulic pressure forces it out at a rate of more than 150 million gallons per day. Some studies indicate that it takes 26 years for the water to travel the 60 miles from the mountains to Giant Springs. Other data suggest that it might be closer to a 50-year journey before it emerges and forms the Roe River.

However, some of the water is trapped in the underground, where it remains far longer than two-and-a-half decades. Scientists have determined that some of the water has been in the underground for two or three thousand years . . . maybe longer. Instead of flowing out, it stays in the aquifer century after century, millennium after millennium.

The water that travels from the mountains and bursts forth at Giant Springs has a year-round, constant temperature of 54 degrees Fahrenheit. This might seem cold to people in warmer regions of the world, but considering the harsh, bitter conditions of a Montana winter, 54 degrees is quite warm. When outside temperatures get down to 50, 60, and 70 below zero, the water from the springs is more than 100 degrees warmer than the air temperature. On the other hand, during the summer months, when the outside temperature reaches to more than 100 degrees Fahrenheit, the cool waters from the springs are rather refreshing.

Most of the water stays underground and doesn't make the journey to Giant Springs. Instead, it combines with streams from the Black Hills, the Big Horn Mountains, and the wider drainage area. Eventually, most of it surfaces in Canada. But some of the water never escapes. It's still trapped, still hidden, still invisible.

I look at this underground water system is an allegory about what happens in people's lives. There's a lot going on inside of us, perhaps a whole lot more than most of us are willing to admit to ourselves or allow others to know about. Because of past, painful experiences, we force our thoughts and emotions underground, and they become an internal, invisible force. It may be hidden, but it's moving. It's active. In fact, sometimes what's going on inside takes on a life of its own, until one day, it gushes out in destructive words or actions, and everybody says things like, "Wow. I never saw that coming." Others are trapped in pain, decade after decade, while life, happiness, and opportunities pass them by. Either by choice or by circumstance, their issues never surface and are never resolved.

The Holy Spirit is ready to help with this inner world of invisible forces and hidden issues. He wants to liberate you. You don't have to remain trapped, hidden, or invisible any longer. Its time for a new beginning.

37
THE FINEST HOURS

Last Night, my wife and I went to the local theater to see The Finest Hours. One of the greatest Coast Guard rescue attempts in history. Watching the film, we both wondered if the rescue team would get there in time, or if the men on the sinking oil tanker died. Wondered if the guys on the rescue boat came back alive, or did they drown in the sea.

I was in the Army for 24 years. My dad and brother were career Navy guys. All three of my sons are in the military (Army & Navy). So I have an appreciation for those who serve in all branches of the Armed Forces. I understand the dangers they face, and their willingness to risk their lives for their country. But on a more personal note, their willingness to risk their lives for people day in and day out – not only during war, but many other dangerous circumstances we sometimes find ourselves in.

I like watching films about the risks people take to help others. I appreciate the men and women in our police and fire departments, ambulance drivers and EMTs, and others who face danger in order to save others.

Watching this film made me proud of the people in the U.S. Coast Guard.

If you haven't yet seen it yet, but you plan to watch it, STOP READING RIGHT NOW. Because I want to comment on a deeply significant aspect of the story.

> SPOILER ALERT. SPOILER ALERT.
> SPOILER ALERT.
> OK. YOU'VE BEEN WARNED.
> IF YOU'RE STILL READING,
> DON'T BLAME ME.

In order for the rescue to even happen, there were at least three independent bold decisions that had to be made. Maybe more.

The first was made by Mr. Sybert on the damaged, about-to-sink tanker. Suddenly finding himself to be the ranking crew member, he made a gutsy decision and destroyed the life boat the other men were about to climb into. They hated him for that, but he knew the roiling sea would destroy that lifeboat and that the men would drown long before the rescue effort arrived

The next daring decision was made by Warrant Officer Cluff, the guy in charge of the Chatham

Coast Guard Station. When nobody thought it even possible for the mission to succeed, he ordered his crew to go out in the worst storm on record, find the sinking ship, and come home with the survivors. His own crew and all the townspeople thought he was a fool.

And the third was by Webber himself, the Coastguardsman who led the rescue operation. The odds and the storm were against him. The raging waves nearly destroyed the boat. His mates urged him to turn around. But he made the bold decision to keep going.

You'll have to watch the movie, read the book, or search online to see how it ended. But what fascinates me is our interconnectedness as human beings. Three men made decisions that directly impacted the others. If any one of the three had acted differently, there would be no rescue, no hero, no story. Nobody would have blamed them for taking the safer course of action. Nobody would say they were wrong if they played it safe.

But thirty-two more men would have died. Thirty-two more families devastated by loss. And those three men would have lived out the remainder of their lives wondering what if.

38
SELMA

We watched Selma tonight. It's painful to see the way people mistreat and abuse other human beings. One of the things that struck me while watching the movie was the way many Christian whites were blind to what was happening. Or worse, they participated in the injustice, the hatred, and the cruelty.

And I can't help but wonder if I have a blindness, too. Am I oblivious to injustice in some ways? Are there times when I stand back and watch when I ought to be doing something to make a difference? Do I care about people who are hurting? Do I care enough?

39
ONLY A RECEPTIONIST

Last night, my wife and I watched another episode of the BBC television show, "Call the Midwife." In this segment, the doctor had to be away from the office because of an emergency, and his wife, who functioned as the receptionist, was running the clinic. When the patients realized the doctor was gone, they refused to let her help them because they were totally unaware that she had worked as a nurse for ten years. In their eyes, she was "only a receptionist" and they bolted for the door until a doctor or nurse was there. The next morning, the "receptionist" was dressed in a nurse uniform, and when she opened the door to let the clients in, they saw her as a professional medical caregiver, and accepted her expertise. Even though she was the same person, respect came with the right uniform.

This concept was the basis of John Molloy's 1975

book titled Dress for Success, and the sequel two years later, The Woman's Dress for Success. The average person is highly influenced by other people's outward appearance, and most of us aren't able to see beyond the surface. If people look good on the outside, we think more highly of them. But if their appearance isn't impressive, we think less about them and, too often, we treat them worse.

This interpersonal dynamic can be seen in the Bible, too. In 1st Samuel chapter 16, the Lord told Samuel to go to Bethlehem to anoint one of Jesse's sons to be the new king. When Samuel saw Eliab, he was impressed, and thought this must be the young man who would be king. But the Lord said to Samuel in a now-famous verse, "People look at the outward appearance, but the Lord looks at the heart."

It seems people of every generation have to re-learn this lesson. It took a vision from the Lord to bring Peter to the point of admitting that "God shows no partiality." James had to remind the church not to treat wealthy people better than the poor when he wrote, "My brothers and sisters, believers in Jesus Christ must not show favoritism."

It's important for us to dress appropriately for work and business appointments. It does make a difference how people see us and think about us. But Christians are called to be different. We can grow in our relationship with Christ and ask the Holy Spirit to help us see people through His eyes, to see beyond the outward appearance and see the heart, the real person. We are called to treat all people with dignity and respect, no matter who they are or what they look like.

The apostle Paul tells Timothy not to let anyone look down on him because he is young. I think it would be fair to replace "young" with a number of other possible factors. Don't let anyone look down on you because you are poor, darker skinned, an immigrant, a woman, a senior citizen, or unemployed. The apostle continues, "Instead, set an example by the way you live and the way you conduct yourself."

Only a receptionist? Only a teen? Only a woman? Only an immigrant? Only a farmer? When I mentor people, I remind them never to use the word "only" when talking about themselves or others. As Christians and as human beings, we have an opportunity to get beyond superficial appearances and circumstances when it comes to how we treat people and how we value them.

40
SHOW ME THE MONEY

Some men tried to set a trap for Jesus one day by asking him a trick question. Is it right to pay taxes to Caesar? They expected a simple yes/no, either/or answer that would force him into a corner and get him into trouble with either the Roman authorities or the Jewish leaders. It would be a win/win for them and a lose/lose for him. But as he often did, Jesus had an interesting reply—Show Me the Money!

"Show Me the coin used for the tax." So they brought Him a denarius.

"Whose image and inscription is this?" He asked them.

"Caesar's," they said to Him.

Then He said to them, "Therefore give back to Caesar the things that are Caesar's, and to God the things that are God's" (Matthew 22:19-22).

In answering their question, Jesus avoided the obvious either/or, and totally reframed the dilemma. In the eternal scheme of things, it doesn't matter who you pay taxes to. The real issue is whose likeness is on the coin and whose picture is on you as a person because the image shows the identity of the owner. Since Caesar's picture is on the denarius, go ahead and return it to him. It belongs to him. Likewise, because God's image is on you, he claims ownership of your life, so give back to the Lord what is rightfully his. You belong to him.

Jesus's reply turned the tables on them because they were the spiritual leaders who were supposed to understand the scriptures. They were the ones who claimed to have the image of God. Yet in reality, they were far from God.

> Give back to Caesar
> what already belongs to him,
> and give back to the Lord
> what already belongs to him.

An adult insect is officially called an imago, which means image or picture. This is the stage the butterfly looks its best, is fully developed, and fulfills its purpose. This is the stage that has captured the imagination of people around the world since the beginning of history. And this is where our discussion of the butterfly life cycle comes to a crescendo.

The butterfly is a wonderful analogy of the

spiritual growth among Christians because metamorphosis means transformation, and the gradual changes from one stage to the next are so appropriate for a discussion of the changes that take place in our lives. But another fantastic part of the story is that the mature or perfect form of the adult butterfly is called an imago. This is a powerful reminder that every human being was fashioned in the Image of God. Theologians refer to this by using the Latin phrase, Imago Dei.

His image, his likeness, his stamp of ownership is indelibly printed on our soul, our very being, and we can choose to give ourselves back to him. This is what we were created for. This is our reason for being. This is what empowers us to reach our highest level of existence. This is what we were designed for.

No matter who you are, where you are from, whether you are male or female, or what you look like, you are made in the Image of God and there's nobody in the world more important or more valuable than you. You are free to be yourself, free to pursue your dreams, free to express yourself, and free to fly. And in that freedom, you can liberate others to do the same. You are special. And you are beautiful.

41
WATERING THE PINEAPPLE

Three or four years ago, a friend gave me the top of a pineapple his family had eaten. He told me, "Plant this in dirt and it'll grow. It sometimes takes a few years, and doesn't even need a whole lot of water."

So I put the thing in a plastic grocery bag, put it in the garage, and forgot about it. A year-and-a-half later while cleaning the garage, I found the parched pineapple top and assumed it was dead. But then I thought, "Why not put it in a pot with some soil and see what happens?" I started watering my experiment once in a while, and after a few months, new life sprouted. When it got to about 20 inches tall, I transplanted it in the back yard. Within another few months there was a pineapple growing in the center of the plant.

There are times when it seems like your marriage is dried up or dead. It might have been months or even years since you've paid attention or invested in the relationship with the one you used to love and care about the most.

But it's not necessarily over. It's not too late to plant new seeds of love and kindness, to offer a timely word of encouragement, or to start "watering the pineapple."

If you decide to start fresh, you'll need to be patient. My pineapple had been dried up and discarded for over a year, and when finally planted, it took months to begin to sprout, and then another year or more before the fruit appeared. It just takes time. Sometimes a lot of time.

It is just as likely that when you begin to express loving, healing thoughts and words, it might take a while before you start to see new life in your marriage. So be patient. Keep on investing in your marriage. Continue loving. Be genuinely interested in your mate's well-being. It's going to be hard at first, but if you are willing to hang in there and continue treating each other right, your marriage can be restored.

Several years ago, we went through a pretty rough time in our marriage. We didn't like each other. We were pretty unhappy. Things weren't going well. I came home from work one day and my wife asked me out of the blue, "Are we ever going to be happy again."

"I don't know, Sweetheart," I answered. And I really didn't. "How 'bout if we just try to be nice to each other, don't do anything that we'd come to regret, and see what happens."

Six or seven months later, we could tell that the joy had returned to our lives. We could smile at each other. We could laugh together. We enjoyed being in the same room. But it didn't happen automatically, and it didn't happen fast. We had to invest in each other, and we had to be patient.

Perhaps you've discarded the idea that you can be happy, or that you can have a good marriage. That pineapple in my backyard is a good reminder that even when things look lifeless, there's still hope. You can reignite the love and the joy in your marriage too.

42
STRAWBERRY PIE

One day my mother-in-law was invited to a social event, a wedding shower I think, and one of the desserts was strawberry pie. This was one of her favorites, and her mouth watered as she prepared for that first bite. The top of the pie was covered with a sweet, red glaze that not only ensured that every bite would be delicious, but also provided a consistent color.

Then something went terribly wrong. When she stabbed the first "strawberry" with her fork, placed it in her mouth, and bit into it, ecstasy turned into horror. What she had in her mouth was not a piece of fruit, but a chunk of manure that had somehow been harvested with the berries, ending up in the pie, camouflaged by that glaze.

The flavor filled her mouth and attacked every taste bud. Bitter. Sour. Nasty. Horrible.

Sin is like that. It looks so good. We've tasted it

before, and it was delicious every time. But ecstasy turns into horror. It doesn't stay sweet forever. It's like that manure, posing as a strawberry, just waiting for the right moment to reveal itself. And when it does, it brings bitterness and pain. Its destruction is horrible. It's impact on a person, a marriage, or a family is sometimes irreversible and irreparable.

Mother never again had a piece of strawberry pie. The experience was too traumatic, and she never wanted to face the possibility of that happening again . . . Ever.

If only we had the same determination to avoid sin.

43
GOD IS OUR HELPER

You can probably think of several characters in TV shows, comic books, movies, and novels who have a sidekick. There are lots of them: Sherlock Holmes and Dr. Watson, Batman and Robin, The Lone Ranger and Tonto, Han Solo and Chewbacca, Don Quixote and Sancho Panza, Andy Griffith and Barney Fife, Captain Kirk and Spock, Robinson Crusoe and Friday, Robin Hood and Little John, Shrek and Donkey, Moses and Aaron, Paul and Silas.

It seems almost every hero has a sidekick who provides comic relief, but also offers serious friendship and assistance along the way. It's a classic technique in literature and drama, where sidekicks play an important role. They help the main character reach his or her goals and accomplish the mission. They offer friendship and provide insight. Usually, they perform tasks that are beneath the dignity of the hero. Sometimes they serve as a contrasting personality. The sidekick may be a commoner or a bumbler, allowing the audience someone they can relate with. Usually, the sidekick isn't quite as smart, but helps the star come up with brilliant ideas. Always, the sidekick is of lesser importance.

A lot of people think of a helper as someone who is less important, less skilled, or less capable than the person who really matters. In our culture, a helper is considered an underling, a hireling, or a subordinate. We call them gophers. We even talk about the hired help—people who do the tasks the important people don't want to do or don't have time to do. Words like assistant, adjunct, apprentice, deputy, and sidekick come to mind.

However, that's not the biblical concept of help. The Hebrew word for helper in the Old Testament is ezer, and comes from a verb that means to rescue, deliver, or help. Whenever it's used of human beings, it's talking about someone who is bigger, stronger, more powerful, smarter, or richer who reaches out to the weak or needy.

Most often, the word refers to God himself. The psalmist wrote, "God is my helper; the Lord is the sustainer of my life" (Psalm 54:4) and "God is our refuge and strength, a helper who is always found in times of trouble" (Psalm 46:1).

The point is that helping people is what God does. He's always ready, willing, and able to help us in our time of need. No wonder Hebrews 4:16 encourages us to "approach God's throne of grace with confidence, so that we may receive mercy and find grace to help us in our time of need (NIV).

Do you need help? Are you struggling at this point in your life? Have you felt like quitting or giving up? Let me encourage you, instead, to turn to the Lord and enter into his presence with confidence. You will find the help you need. That's what God does. That's who he is.

44
FIRST BREATH

A newborn whale swims instinctively towards the surface;
Within ten seconds, it must breathe or die.
Some get there in time, take that breath, and life begins—
Swimming with Mom, giving and receiving affection, diving and playing
Ready to grow and learn and be.

But sometimes the calf doesn't surface
Or needs help, or manages to get there, but doesn't inhale.
If a newborn human doesn't breathe right away
A doctor, a nurse, or a midwife may startle it by slapping it on the thigh
Or the air passage might need to be cleared.

A mother humpback has some tricks up her sleeve,

too.
Scientists, photographers, kayakers, surfers, and tourists have observed
A mother assisting her calf take that all-important first breath.
She noses her child, or swims under her babe so it's lying across her head
And carries it upward.

Making sure the infant's face stays above water until it breathes
Because until that happens, life's not guaranteed.
One pair of researchers happened upon a whale as she was giving birth;
The calf's flippers tight against its body, pinned to its sides,
It hadn't moved or breathed, and seemed to be in trouble.

Its eyes sealed shut, lungs still dormant,
They watched as the mother whale went under, then lifted her baby
And held it at the surface, blow hole in the sunlight.
They heard her making sounds, as if reassuring her baby, singing a lullaby, coaxing it to breathe.
Suddenly, the newborn gasped, air filled the lungs, eyes opened, pectoral fins extended.

Mama knew her child was okay.

45
WALKING THE BEAGLE

While taking a walk one afternoon, the Beagle stops and stares out into a vacant field of grass about fourteen or fifteen inches high, and stares for a long time. Then she makes a sharp turn to the left, straight into the emptiness. Nothing but tall grass, as far as I can tell. About fifty feet from the road she stops, raises one paw, and waits. And waits. Having no appointments or reason to hurry today, I decide to let her do whatever it is she thinks she wants to do. I glance at my watch. Two, three, four, five minutes go by. She is frozen, looking straight down into the grass. Six, seven, eight, nine minutes. That's a long time to stand there looking at the grass, dog.

Suddenly, she lunges, her snout, face, and head disappearing into the sea of green. When she finally comes up for air, there's a huge rat in her mouth. She looks up at me as if to say, See? I knew it was there. And you doubted me! Are you proud of me?

GOTCHA

The Beagle suddenly transforms into the Mighty Hunter, triumphantly prancing around with that rodent dangling from both sides of her jowls, writhing to see if there's any chance of freeing itself from the jaws of death. Nope. Not a chance.

This is first blood for the Beagle, and our walks are never the same. Prior to catching that rat in the field, she frequently stopped to sniff the air, detecting something that the oblivious human at the end of the leash was unable to sense. But her new experience gives her confidence. Now, she understands what it means to smell a rat.

From now on, there's no such thing as going for a walk. The Beagle is out for a hunt, tugging and pulling and motivated.

Though she has excellent hearing and vision, the nose is primarily how she encounters and understands her world. Like other hounds, the Beagle can detect the scent of another animal up to seven days later. For this reason, going out for a walk is her equivalent of reading the morning newspaper or watching the evening news. She waits every day for me to put on my walking shoes, slip on the sunglasses, pick up the leash, and let a new adventure begin.

46
ANCIENT CANINE RITUAL

I go out to the garage to get something, and my little shadow, follows me. As I'm turning to go back into the house, I notice that she sees something interesting over in the corner. When I turn off the light and call her, she runs past me as fast as she can go, into the living room, and hides. Following her, I see that she has a new "toy." The interesting thing she saw in the garage was a frog.

Now, Sophie knows that whenever she comes into the house with a critter, I always take it from her. But she doesn't want to lose this frog, so now the chase is on.

I call for back-up. "Help!" and my wife and I corner the dog in my office, frog still in mouth. Then, as she reaches towards the Beagle . . . Gulp! That frog is G-O-N-E!

On the treadmill one afternoon, I look out the window just in time to see a giant lizard appear over the top of the back wall. Lizards frequently come into the yard to sun themselves on our deck, or to go underneath it. This lizard was big. No, not an alligator, not even an iguana. Just your ordinary Florida lizard. But to get this size, he had to live long, eat well, and prosper. And avoid cars, trucks, birds, and other predators.

So the big fat grand-daddy-of-a-lizard comes into the domain of the Beagle. I imagine he never met a dog before. At least not one like Sophie. Sophie loves lizards. Loves to toy with them. Loves to catchem and eatem. Well, the top half of 'em anyway. I often find half-lizards lying around the house. I never knew a lizard had blood before the Beagle joined the family.

About the time I see Grandaddy, so does Sophie, and she's making a Beagle-line to the back wall. The chase is on. Not much of a chase. A grampa lizard verses a Beagle-in-her-prime? Soon Sophie is prancing. Head up, high-stepping around the yard, smiling. She tosses the crocodilian and then chases it again. Puts one paw on it to hold it down. When she's certain that it is immobilized, she goes into the Spinning Nose Dive, otherwise known as her version of the touchdown dance.

If you've ever seen Snoopy do the Happy Dance in the Peanuts comic strip or the televised cartoon, well, that's exactly what a Beagle does. Only upside down on the ground. Every time she catches a lizard or a bug, she does the nose dive into the grass and proceeds to roll around on top of it. The lizard is no more. The Beagle lives another day.

Must be some sort of ancient Canine Ritual.

When my friend, Adam, lived in Brooklyn, his dog did the Canine Ritual on heaps of barnacles and stenching, piled-up-on-the-beach stuff. Just rolled around on the rotting rubble, making sure his fur smelled just the same as the putrefying sea creatures on the beach.

47
WHAT IT MEANS TO BE A MAN

One night after we go to bed, Sophie the Beagle goes outside, presumably to relieve herself, before settling down for the night. But instead of coming back into the house, she's out in the back yard for a long time. Then she starts baying, barking, and bawling like members of her breed are known to do. Neighbors on both sides have told me they can hear her when she does that, so I go to the back door and call to her, but she won't come in. I go back to bed. Her noise continues, however, so I go back out to see what's happening. There's Sophie, dancing in the moonlight, circling a designated spot in the grass. Singing and laughing. It's dark and I don't have my glasses on, so I stoop down to see if she has a lizard, but something bigger than a lizard moves in the grass. What is it, a frog? While my eyes are trying to focus, the creature stands up trying to defend itself from its predator. It's not a frog . . . not unless frogs in Florida have mutated and morphed into four-footed, furry things.

I go back into the house to tell my wife, "I think Sophie has a mole or a gopher."

"Go kill it!" was her reply.

"I think Sophia can do a fine job of that," I bravely retort. "My concern is that she might bring it into the house to play with it and show us."

So, I close the doggie door, locking Sophie out, and climb back into bed. But we can't sleep, and neither can the neighbors.

"You're the man. Go out there and kill it!"

Well, if that's the definition of manhood, I better get to it! So, I bravely say to my wife, "I'll go kill the thing if you go with me!" Definitely the manly way to approach the situation.

We both put on our slippers, I find the flashlight, then go to the garage and get a shovel. A flat shovel, not a rounded one, mind you. Husband and wife now return to the scene of the crime, Beagle still playing and singing "Ring Around the Rosie" with the wild thing.

"Do you want me to hold the light?" my accomplice asks.

"Yes, that's a good idea."

She shines the light on a medium-sized mole. As Sophie sits down to catch her breath and look at her new toy, I whack it with the shovel. The rodent, not the Beagle. Then I whack it again, scoop it up, and toss it over the back wall. Sophie spends the next hour looking for it. Then she comes in, and we all sleep through the night.

GOTCHA

The next morning, I notice a committee of vultures circling overhead. By the time I finish breakfast and manage to look over the wall an hour or so later, the carrion-eaters had finished their meal, leaving no traces of the previous night's adventure.

ACKNOWLEDGEMENTS

I want to thank the editors, publishers, and magazines who published many of the pieces in this collection.

CBN Online Devotionals
Army Magazine, Association of the U. S. Army.
Morgan James Publishing
Wipf & Stock Publishing
WisdomBuilt® Books
Senior Living Magazine, Asbury Press
EA Books
Mountain Movers Magazine
Perhaps one or two others I cannot remember

ABOUT THE AUTHOR

Paul Linzey was a pastor before becoming an Army chaplain, and retired from the military in 2015 at the rank of Colonel. He and his wife planted Friendship Church, which is in Mulberry, FL, and then he taught full-time at Southeastern University in Lakeland, FL, where he is still an adjunct professor of Practical Ministry and a mentor in their Doctor of Ministry program.

When he became the Protestant pastor at the United States Naval Academy in Annapolis, Maryland, in a sense, he was returning to the Blue Side and coming full circle because he grew up in a Navy family. His father and brother were Navy chaplains, and one of his sons is currently a Navy chaplain. His other two sons are Army officers.

Linzey is an award-winning author who has written articles for religious and military magazines. Many of his devotional articles can be seen at CBN.org's online magazine. He was a contributing writer and editor for Life Publisher's Warriors Bible in 2014. In 2019 he self-published a book called WisdomBuilt: Biblical Principles of Marriage. His second book, released in 2020, has a foreword by Dr. Richard Blackaby and is titled Safest Place in Iraq. The book focuses on his experience as a military chaplain in Iraq during the war. His third book, Military Ministry: Chaplains in the Twenty-First

Century, was co-written with Dr. Keith Travis, professor of practical ministry and chaplaincy at Liberty University.

Linzey completed the Bachelor of Arts in Religious Studies at Vanguard University in Costa Mesa, CA. Graduate degrees include the Master of Divinity from Fuller Theological Seminary, the Doctor of Ministry at Gordon-Conwell Theological Seminary, and an MFA in Creative Writing at the University of Tampa. He taught Creative Writing at Southeastern University, and has been a featured speaker at several writers conferences and workshops.

Throughout his adult life, whether serving in a church, the military, or the university, he has been involved in small group ministries, pastoral care, lay leadership training, and marriage/family seminars and retreats.

Interests include music, digital photography, movies and theater, sports, and family. He and his wife have three sons and ten grandchildren.

His theme scripture is First Thessalonians 2:8, We loved you so much that we were willing to share with you not only the gospel of God but our lives as well, because you had become so dear to us.

Linzey's website/blog is paullinzey.com. In addition, he can be found on Facebook and LinkedIn.

Books by Paul E. Linzey

Fiction

Bekker's Burial
You Never Know
Twist of Fate

Nonfiction

Safest Place in Iraq
Butterfly Believers
Gotcha
Military Ministry
WisdomBuilt: Biblical Principles of Marriage

Contributing Author or Editor

The Warrior's Bible
Reflections: An Anthology of Memoir & Short Story
Dead in the Water: The USS Yorktown at Midway
Looking Through the Rearview Mirror
Reflections Along the Journey
Getting it Twisted
Echoes from the Same House

GOTCHA

www.ingramcontent.com/pod-product-compliance
Lightning Source LLC
Chambersburg PA
CBHW060323050426
42449CB00011B/2622